Everybody
Needs
an Editor

Everybody Needs an Editor

The Essential Guide
to Clear and Effective Writing

Melissa Harris and Jenn Bane
Edited by Mark Jacob

Simon Element

New York • London • Toronto • Sydney • New Delhi

SIMON
ELEMENT

An Imprint of Simon & Schuster, LLC
1230 Avenue of the Americas
New York, NY 10020

First Simon Element hardcover edition September 2024

SIMON ELEMENT is a trademark of Simon & Schuster, LLC

Simon & Schuster: Celebrating 100 Years of Publishing in 2024

For information about special discounts for bulk purchases, please contact Simon & Schuster Special Sales at 1-866-506-1949 or business@simonandschuster.com.

The Simon & Schuster Speakers Bureau can bring authors to your live event. For more information or to book an event, contact the Simon & Schuster Speakers Bureau at 1-866-248-3049 or visit our website at www.simonspeakers.com.

Interior design by Laura Levatino

Manufactured in China

10 9 8 7 6 5 4 3 2 1

Library of Congress Cataloging-in-Publication Data has been applied for.

ISBN 978-1-6680-1729-6
ISBN 978-1-6680-1730-2 (ebook)

To Jane Hirt,
true believer

Contents

2. Let's Top It

Getting Opened

Getting Noticed

3. Let's Format It

Organization for Emphasis

How to Make Your Communication Look, Feel, and Sound Better

4. Let's Fix It

Advice on What to Do—and Not Do— for Effective Communication

Clichés and Other Common Blunders

Everybody Needs an Editor

Introduction

We're irritated.

Our main grievance: writing that is too long, too cluttered, and too littered with jargon, acronyms, and highfalutin words. Like that one. "Highfalutin." Terrible.

Over my fifteen-year journalism career, I committed many crimes against language, but editors at places like the *Chicago Tribune*, the *Baltimore Sun*, *Orlando Sentinel*, and the *Indianapolis Star* bailed me out.

After leaving journalism, I launched a marketing agency with other newsroom veterans. As the company grew, I spent far less time writing, and far more time tightening others' work—everything from annual reports to billboards.

I started to joke that we were in the liposuction business because we were cutting so much text.

Too often, we must coax writers to accept slimmer versions. We have to persuade them that direct, clear writing is not "dumbing it down." Instead, it demonstrates respect for your audience; it seizes their attention—and keeps it.

Some people will turn to generative AI for this job. It can quickly produce clean writing. It also loves clichés and hates fact-checking.

So read on, and you'll learn to upgrade an algorithm's first draft, if not dump the AI altogether. You'll learn to enliven your work. You might even have edits for this very book. Email us—we can take it.

With gratitude,

Melissa Harris

M. Harris & Co. founder
melissa@mharris.com

Easy reading is damn hard writing.

—Nathaniel Hawthorne

Chapter 1

Let's Write It

Actually, let's not. Because writers hate writing.
Scratch that—writers hate getting *started* with writing. The blank page is more than intimidating. It provokes night sweats.

So let's begin with a page that isn't blank. Make it not-blank as quickly as possible by answering these five questions:

1. Who is your audience? (Who is this piece of communication for? Your answer should be more specific than "customers" or "clients.")
2. What is it? (A guide? A report? A recap?)
3. What is the goal? (To persuade? To prompt action? If so, what action?)
4. How is it going to achieve this objective?
5. Why does it matter now? (Why are you writing it today, versus a year ago?)

The challenge: Your responses should be just one sentence. If you can't distill your answers, you're not ready to write. You're still in the conceptual phase.

We ask our clients these exact questions before they launch any service or product. It's an exercise that exposes misunderstandings and forces decisions. We even answered them ourselves to write this book:

1. **Who is this book for?** Young professionals entering the workforce; people who think or have been told their writing needs work.
2. **What is it, exactly?** A skimmable writing reference guide.
3. **What's the goal?** To be a resource that readers refer back to often, and that managers gift to their employees.
4. **How will you do that?** By keeping the entries brief and the chapters organized so that readers can quickly find answers to their most common questions.
5. **Why does it matter now?** Because increasingly people think ChatGPT is the answer to poor communication.

Getting started is the hardest part. Now that you've catapulted over the biggest hurdle, let's journey into the four sections of this book—Let's Write It, Let's Top It, Let's Format It, and Let's Fix It—known collectively as WTFF.

Writing Better
Business Communication

Your ability to communicate clearly is key to your professional reputation. If your writing is too formal, your audience will find you stiff. If your writing is too breezy, your audience may not take you seriously. If it's filled with grammatical errors, your audience will think you're an idiot.

A raise often hangs on your ability to write well and convey your meaning.

No pressure.

Pitch Perfectly

Let's write your elevator pitch.

An elevator pitch is a short story about yourself. Everyone can benefit from having one ready. An elevator pitch allows you to make swift and confident introductions (in person or in writing). It can also act as a foundation for interviews, cover letters, or sales calls.

Your pitch should be brief enough to deliver to someone while riding between floors on an elevator. (Notice we didn't say delivered to someone *trapped with you* on an elevator. This isn't an aggressive hard sell.)

To get comfortable saying your pitch out loud, start by writing it. Here's how:

- **Summarize yourself in one intriguing sentence.** Lead with your highest-level self-description, like that you're a former accountant now teaching math to unruly kids, a retired naval officer who suffered bad seasickness, or a stylist on a mission to make people like everything in their closet.

- **Nail the grippy details.** A successful elevator pitch invites—*demands*—a follow-up question. You just said you're an oil industry project manager who's worked in every country that starts with the letter *N*. Now we have to know: Which did you like better, New Zealand or Nepal?

- **Do more than spout your résumé.** As in storytelling, your pitch should have narrative flow. Use an anecdote to sum up your experience, or tell your tale in chronological order: After a lifetime of investigative journalism, you're about to publish your first detective novel.

- **Practice it out loud.** Use a timer. Get it as close to thirty seconds as possible.

- **Be mindful about name-dropping.** Mentioning specific people or places boosts credibility, but if you immediately list five celebrity pals, you won't come across as successful. You will come across as a blowhard.

An example:

I'm the founder and CEO of a Chicago marketing firm whose job is to make our clients unforgettable. We joke that we're actually in the liposuction business; we cut jargon and extra words out of most everything we touch.

Our clients are well-known institutions, such as the American Academy of Pediatrics and the University of Chicago, and the firm has taken off because we relentlessly pursue exceptional talent: Pulitzer, James Beard, and even Grammy Award winners.

I got my start in journalism, as did most of the team. That means we know how to capture an audience's attention—and hold it.

Stand Out on Social Media

Social media is like a playground of screaming children: It's hard to get a word in. And it's always evolving. What gets attention now may not in six months. Here's some advice that won't expire:

- **Know your intent.** What're you trying to do? Educate? Get people to sign up for your newsletter? RSVP for an event? Knowing this first will help guide the focus. Give clear marching orders on what you want your reader to do next.

- **Bring the social to social media.** Ask never-heard-before questions. Invite comments and conversation. (This will also drive up your engagement metrics, which bosses love.)

- **Make it glanceable.** To get your posts read, make them easy to read. No one likes seeing a block of text. Add spaces between paragraphs, or better yet, don't write paragraphs. Write in bullet points. And don't be afraid to throw in an emoji every now and again. 😉

- **Know your voice.** Are you playful? Bold? Optimistic? Decide on your adjectives and stick to them. Think of what will resonate most with the audience you're trying to reach.

For many of our clients, this is the toughest one. They're often too cautious or afraid to build a truly distinct voice. Jenn was the first hire at Cards Against Humanity and managed their acidic social media accounts for years.

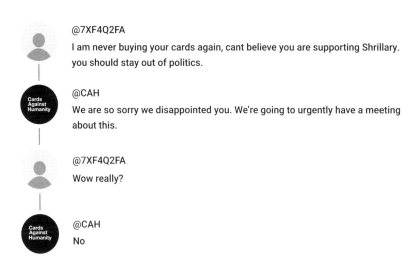

@7XF4Q2FA
I am never buying your cards again, cant believe you are supporting Shrillary. you should stay out of politics.

@CAH
We are so sorry we disappointed you. We're going to urgently have a meeting about this.

@7XF4Q2FA
Wow really?

@CAH
No

You can't break through on social media with content that is dull, and if you have no choice but to be dull, you or your company shouldn't spend much time or effort here.

Here's another example. It's a tweet by Big Bird from *Sesame Street*:

@BigBird
I got the COVID-19 vaccine today! My wing is feeling a little sore, but it'll give my body an extra protective boost that keeps me and others healthy. Ms. @EricaRHill even said I've been getting vaccines since I was a little bird. I had no idea!

This tweet has a voice, a purpose, and it's punchy. It also happens to be adorable. Hits all the marks.

How to Write Work Emails That Won't Make Your Coworkers Hate You

Know this: The second you hit send on an email, you lose control of your audience. You don't get to decide who sees it next.

With that terrifying thought in mind, here's what not to do in work emails:

- **Don't write anything you wouldn't want to see screenshot and then posted on social media, or forwarded to your mom or to us.** Email feels fleeting, but it's forever. So don't bad-mouth your boss in writing. Do it in person instead!

- **Don't write a long series of paragraphs.** You know how people sometimes say that a meeting could have been an email? Well, the opposite is also true. People don't read long emails, so don't write them.

- **Consolidate your emails whenever possible.** It's better to send someone one email with three short topics than three separate emails. But if you do that, number the topics so your recipient won't overlook one of them.

- **Don't ask for a raise in an email.** Instead, ask for a meeting. Yes, you should state that the purpose of said meeting is to discuss a possible raise, but save the negotiations for face-to-face. If you think it's easier to make your case in writing, consider that it's also easier for your boss to say no in writing.

- **Don't quit over email.** Deliver the news in person if at all possible, or on Zoom if it isn't. If you're parting on friendly terms, a brief conversation with your supervisor gives both of you a chance to reflect on your work together and to say thanks. If not, then at least you don't come across as spineless, because you aren't. And speaking of spineless, here's a corollary tip for bosses: Don't fire an employee via email.

- **Don't use reply all with large groups—unless you've got the absolute funniest one-liner of all time.** We're talking a real zinger.

Bcc: Are You Sure?

When you send something to someone through bcc, you might think you're protecting privacy, but are you also compromising the trust of the bcc'd?

Your cloaked friends may wonder how often you do this, and why. And whether you put others on bcc in emails to them.

If you can't be transparent, communicate in another way.

But consider this exception to the "don't use bcc" rule.

If you're blasting many recipients, bcc protects the privacy of your contacts. It also saves people the time it takes to scroll through the mailing list.

Still, use it sparingly.

How to Deliver Bad Work News

When you're delivering really bad news, you should do it in person, not in writing. But since this is a book about writing, let's take an example where an email might be appropriate.

Say your company is closing a branch office, a move that suggests sales are down and some jobs might be in peril. You have to write a memo to the staff.

First, for an example of what not to do, here's a real email Micro-soft employees received in 2014, which was covered in the media and you can easily find online.

Hello there,

Microsoft's strategy is focused on productivity and our desire to help people "do more." As the Microsoft Devices Group, our role is to light up this strategy for people. We are the team creating the hardware that showcases the finest of Microsoft's digital work and digital life experiences, and we will be the confluence of the best of Microsoft's applications, operating systems and cloud services.

To align with Microsoft's strategy, we plan to focus our efforts. Given the wide range of device experiences, we must concentrate on the areas where we can add the most value. The roots of this company and our future are in productivity and helping people get things done. Our fundamental focus— for phones, Surface, for meetings with devices like PPI, Xbox hardware and new areas of innovation—is to build on that strength. While our direction in the majority of our teams is largely unchanging, we have had an opportunity to plan carefully about the alignment of phones within Microsoft as the transferring Nokia team continues with its integration process.

It is particularly important to recognize that the role of phones within Microsoft is different than it was within Nokia. Whereas the hardware business of phones within Nokia was an end unto itself, within Microsoft all our devices are intended to embody the finest of Microsoft's digital work and digital life experiences, while accruing value to Microsoft's overall strategy. Our device strategy must reflect Microsoft's strategy and must be accomplished within an appropriate financial envelope. Therefore, we plan to make some changes.

We will be particularly focused on making the market for Windows Phone. In the near term, we plan to drive Windows Phone volume by targeting the more affordable smartphone segments, which are the fastest growing segments of the market, with Lumia. In addition to the portfolio already planned, we plan to deliver additional lower-cost Lumia devices by shifting select future Nokia X designs and products to Windows Phone devices. We expect to make this shift immediately while continuing to sell and support existing Nokia X products.

To win in the higher price segments, we will focus on delivering great breakthrough products in alignment with major milestones ahead from both the Windows team and the Applications and Services Group. We will ensure that the very best experiences and scenarios from across the company will be showcased on our products. We plan to take advantage of innovation from the Windows team, like Universal Windows Apps, to continue to enrich the Windows application ecosystem. And in the very lowest price ranges, we plan to run our first phones business for maximum efficiency with a smaller team.

We expect these changes to have an impact to our team structure. With our focus, we plan to consolidate the former Smart Devices and Mobile Phones business units into one phone business unit that is responsible for all of our phone efforts. Under the plan, the phone business unit will be led by Jo Harlow with key members from both the Smart Devices and Mobile Phones teams in the management team. This team will be responsible for the success of our Lumia products, the transition of select future Nokia X products to Lumia and for the ongoing operation of the first phone business.

As part of the effort, we plan to select the appropriate business model approach for our sales markets while continuing to offer our products in all markets with a strong focus on maintaining business continuity. We will determine each market approach based on local market dynamics, our ability to profitably deliver local variants, current Lumia momentum and the strategic importance of the market to Microsoft. This will all be balanced with our overall capability to invest.

Our phone engineering efforts are expected to be concentrated in Salo, Finland (for future, high-end Lumia products) and Tampere, Finland (for more affordable devices). We plan to develop the supporting technologies in both locations. We plan to ramp down engineering work in Oulu. While we plan to reduce the engineering in Beijing and San Diego, both sites will continue to have supporting roles, including affordable devices in Beijing and supporting specific US requirements in San Diego. Espoo and Lund are planned to continue to be focused on application software development.

We plan to right-size our manufacturing operations to align to the new strategy and take advantage of integration opportunities. We expect to focus phone production mainly in Hanoi, with some production to continue in Beijing and Dongguan. We plan to shift other Microsoft manufacturing and repair operations to Manaus and Reynosa respectively, and start a phased exit from Komaron, Hungary.

In short, we will focus on driving Lumia volume in the areas where we are already successful today in order to make the market for Windows Phone. With more speed, we will build on our success in the affordable smartphone space with new products offering more differentiation. We'll focus on acquiring new customers in the markets where Microsoft's services and products are most concentrated. And, we'll continue building momentum around applications

<u>We plan that this would result in an estimated reduction of 12,500 factory direct and professional employees over the next year.</u> These decisions are difficult for the team, and we plan to support departing team members with severance benefits. More broadly across the Devices team, we will continue our efforts to bring iconic tablets to market in ways that complement our OEM partners, power the next generation of meetings & collaboration devices and thoughtfully expand Windows with new interaction models.

With a set of changes already implemented earlier this year in these teams, this means there will be limited change for the Surface, Xbox hardware, PPI/meetings or next generation teams. We recognize these planned changes are broad and have very difficult implications for many of our team members. We will work to provide as much clarity and information as possible. Today and over the coming weeks leaders across the organization will hold town halls, host information sharing sessions and provide more details on the intranet.

We know you didn't read that, so we'll summarize: It took eleven paragraphs until layoffs were even mentioned.

Here's how to handle this less clumsily than Microsoft:

- **Don't make your email a guessing game.** Deliver the bad news clearly and directly in the first two sentences.

- **Don't explain to them why this news is really not so bad, don't give misleading explanations, and don't make promises you can't keep.** You'll be accused of being a liar later.

- **Acknowledge their concerns.** Stay positive, but stay honest, too.

- **Keep it vanilla.** Don't be clever. Avoid adjectives and adverbs that might be seized upon by people who are upset. Read over the memo three times looking for phrases that might set people off.

- **Don't get personal and say something like, "As a ten-year veteran of the company, I feel especially bad about this."** No one cares.

Now, here's an example of a direct, compassionate email:

Staff—

We have some bad news: We'll be closing the Centerville office as of June 30 because of lagging sales. Our colleagues who work there will be transferred to our main office, so please make them feel welcome.

I'd like to assure you that no staff reductions are anticipated at this time, and I'll point to the fact that we're launching a new product next month as a sign that we're upbeat about the future.

A business like ours relies on the teamwork and creative ideas of all of us. So if you have any suggestions, questions, or concerns, please contact me to discuss them.

When we work together, we succeed.

—The boss

No sugarcoating, no burying the critical information. But it does cite a piece of positive news and tries to maintain an optimistic attitude. (A lot of this advice works for in-person deliveries of bad news, too.)

How to Give Constructive Writing Feedback

When you give feedback about a colleague's writing, you should tell the truth. But it shouldn't be the unvarnished truth. Use a *little* varnish. Like so:

> Hank,
>
> I took a look at the "About Us" you drafted for the website. I love the way you describe our company's mission. That's a message we have to get across better to both our customers and our own staff. I wouldn't change a thing about that sentence. It's perfect.
>
> Beyond that, you can do some more trimming. Let's try to get this down to two paragraphs.
>
> Also, have you thought about saying something about us being named "Best Software Company" by that industry group? It was a huge honor, and you know how potential customers love that kind of validation.
>
> Great job.
>
> —Your colleague

- **Find something positive to say.** And lead with it.

- **Be honest, but keep negative comments brief.** Don't go on and on, because that feeds the normal human instinct to be defensive.

- **To avoid scolding, advise your colleagues to read their own work aloud.** Any point at which they get tongue-tied, they should rework or cut.

- **Don't be too picky.** If you're asked for your opinion on a piece of text that will be released publicly, try to find out whether another editor will read it before it's released. If so, you don't have to get into the weeds about every little thing, like whether a closed-quote mark is backward. A long line of picky corrections can be soul-killing to the recipient and can also diminish the impact of your top-line feedback.

- **Give the person a chance to fix their own problems.** For example, if it's a first draft, suggest what they might add or delete. Don't rewrite the whole thing right away. Give them a chance to get it right and retain the pride of authorship.

The goal is to make the recipient feel like a collaborator. You're working together to get it right.

Why You Should Use LinkedIn Even Though It's Boring

LinkedIn is the most professional of all major social media platforms. It's also the most boring. It's the conference room of the internet. But that's fine! There are other places we can all hang out, like the family reunion (Facebook) or down in the basement (X).

LinkedIn is useful because of its search engine optimization (SEO) power. When someone googles you, unless you have a common name, your LinkedIn profile will rank high. This is important if you're job hunting. Or better yet, *before* you're job hunting. Building a robust LinkedIn presence *before* you need a new job is like learning to use the fire extinguisher before your stovetop catches fire. It's best to prepare for life's crises before you're under pressure and the stakes are high.

But your presence on LinkedIn is only as good as your profile, connections, and activity.

How to improve your LinkedIn profile:

- **Fill it out completely—all the sections.** Give details in the "Experience" section. This is your résumé.

- **Did you actually remember to put your email address in the "Contact Info" section?** So many people forget this part.

- **Attach examples of your best work.**

- **BCC—Be constantly connecting.** Invite people you've worked with previously and those you aspire to work with.

- **Add a note with your invitation.** Remind them how they know you or explain why you'd like to connect.

- **Consult your calendar monthly and invite everyone you've met with that month.**

- **Post, comment, or like at least once a week.** We know—this is hard. Try to do it anyway. Share links you find interesting, news from your company, work you are proud of.

And when you need a job, people need to know that. No one can read your mind. Tell your network that you are looking for work. Say the kind of job you're looking for and in what city. Encourage them to send you suggestions, job links, and referrals.

Then step back and watch the network you worked so hard to build help you find your next job. LinkedIn is an opportunity to show that you are the kind of person someone else would want to work with.

How to Say Goodbye to Colleagues

Like middle school crushes and fashion trends, colleagues come and go. While these relationships may be strictly business, it's a courteous gesture to bid them a proper farewell. Unless they were awful, in which case, feel free to skip this part and read on.

Here's how to structure a goodbye message:

- **Acknowledge their departure and let them know how it makes you feel.** This could be a congratulatory moment where you are excited for their next chapter or expressing sadness in seeing them leave under unfortunate circumstances.

- **Add a personal touch.** What will you miss about working with this person? Getting coffee? Online shopping? Sneaking out of the office before 5 p.m.? Perhaps you want to let this person know you appreciated working on a collaborative project or thank them for bringing a little more joy to work.

- **Suggest how you'd like to keep in contact.** This is your chance to let your colleague know how comfortable you are with continuing your relationship. You could say:
  - Looking forward to following your successes.
  - Feel free to use me as a reference in the future.
  - Let me know if you'd like to grab lunch after you settle into your new position.

- **Reiterate your best wishes.** Finally, close it all up with one last good luck.

Like so:

Jordan,

I heard the news that you're departing. I'm sad to say farewell to someone so talented, positive, and generous. I especially loved dissecting *The Bachelor* with you every week.

    This is my personal email. Let's get coffee soon so I can hear all about the new gig (and what you think of next season's contestants).

    All the best,
    Carmen

And if you're the one leaving, it's best to make your announcements face-to-face.

Then, your final farewell email can go something like this:

Team,

With this Friday as my last day, I wanted to send a last note of gratitude.

    It's been a joy to work with you all. Thank you for making this company a great place to work. Here's my number to keep in touch . . .

Now, let's say you're leaving on less-than-happy terms. In that case, write the email you wish you could send—the one that's burning in your heart.

Perhaps it goes something like this:

Team,

With this Friday as my last day, I wanted to send one last note of regret. Working with you all has been awful. Each and every one of you has contributed to making this a horrible place to work. If you have my personal phone number, pretend you don't. Let's never talk again.

Then take a deep, cleansing breath—and delete. Don't hit that tempting send button.

If you choose to ignore that advice and hit send anyway, please forward us all responses so we can enjoy the fireworks.

How to Add Warmth to a Cold Email

First rule on cold emails: Try to avoid them. Like this one we received:

Hello, Melissa,

We helped another marketing agency go from $4.3M to $11.3M in just one year by revamping their outbound strategy and completely transforming the way their sales team generates leads and referrals.

We at [Name of Company] are a collective of revenue generation experts who leverage behavioral economics to help businesses optimize their sales methods.

Free this week to learn more about how our tactics can help M. Harris?

Look forward to connecting,

Generic, impersonal. This email says more about what they did for another company, not what they can do for *us* specifically. Whenever possible, have a mutual acquaintance do the introduction for you.

But when you have no choice but to go in cold, make sure you do your homework first. Customize the email. Read public social media feeds. (Scan X or LinkedIn. Nothing creepy.)

Here's an example:

Kimberly,

I'm Jenn, and I'm a producer on a short documentary about Chicago's historic lakefront. We would cherish the opportunity to film an interview with you.

As you know, Chicago's lakefront is all protected public land, with no private beaches. I read your newsletter about city parks belonging to everyone, so we'd love your perspective on just how special our lakefront is.

The details:

- Time commitment is 1 hour.
- We'll record at an outdoor location that's convenient for you and near the lakefront.
- We are aiming to film this month.

Happy to answer your questions.

Thank you for your consideration,
Jenn

How to Make an Email Introduction

When you want to connect two people, especially when one party wants something from the other, ask permission first.

Here's an example that we've slightly doctored to disguise the identity of one of our clients. The context is that we wanted to connect our client to our literary agent, Monika.

> Monika,
>
> I'm writing to seek permission to introduce you to Chef Lydia Kwon. Chef Lydia is a two-Michelin-starred chef. You may have seen her on the new season of *Kitchen Heroes*. As if that's not enough, Lydia also operates a chihuahua rescue here in St. Paul.
>
> Lydia has written an autobiography, which details her challenging upbringing and journey to becoming a world-renowned chef and the director of Lend A Paw. I'm hoping you would be willing to take a call with her and her writing partner.
>
> Is this something you're open to?

Monika said yes. So we replied and added Lydia to the thread. (Before approaching Monika, we got Lydia's sign-off, too.)

Everyone's time is valuable. Don't foist someone on anyone, especially a professional contact.

Honor Vacations

The best way to honor someone's vacation is to leave them alone.

The second-best way is to do a little prep work before they leave.

If you work closely on a team with someone who's going on vacation, ask:

- Is there anything brewing that could become a crisis while you're away?
- Do you want me to let you know if that happens?
- Is there anything else important you would want to know about—that I should interrupt your vacation to tell you?
- How should I contact you? Should I text, call, email?

About email: You may be tempted to keep cc'ing your colleague on daily emails and including them in responses. Don't assume that. It's better to ask what they prefer rather than trying to read their mind.

You could offer to schedule emails for the day they return, or to write one update email at the end of the week instead of forwarding twenty.

And if you yourself are the one trying to get away, be proactive to protect yourself:

- Resist reading work emails on vacation. It's the same as working—and you, my friend, are on vacation.
- Before you go, let important clients or close colleagues know so they can get last-minute questions out of the way.
- Ask a trusted colleague to contact you if something happens that you should know about. Yes, that's vague. And it requires a

colleague to exercise good judgment on whether to bug you. So choose wisely.

- Set an out-of-office notification on your work email and ask a colleague if they would be willing to be an emergency contact.

An example:

I am out of the office this week and will have limited access to email. I will return March 9.

    If your issue is an emergency and requires urgent attention, please contact my colleague Pat Rogers at [Pat's email address].

What you shouldn't do is write your memo like this, even if you want to:

I am out of the office until further notice.

    If your issue is an emergency and requires urgent attention, deal with it yourself.

How to Write a Rejection Letter

Rejection letters aren't fun to receive, and they're not fun to write, either. But you should respond to each person who approaches you about a job. You send rejection letters so you don't leave people wondering, and to maintain your professionalism. No ghosting allowed here.

Here's an example of an email you can copy if you want to make the recipient feel great and then terrible:

Dear Samantha,

Thank you for taking the time to apply to our company. We were impressed with your writing samples, and someone with your passion is exactly what we need more of around here!

But unfortunately we are going in a different direction and hiring a candidate with more experience. We encourage you to apply again in the fall. Good luck pursuing your dreams!

Youch. The reverse Uno card. To ensure you don't come across as patronizing as this message, follow these rules:

- **Be kind.** Thank the candidate, provide an appropriate explanation, and lower the boom.

- **Be succinct.** Getting a two-page rejection letter doesn't feel better than getting a single-paragraph one.

- **Treat it like a legal document.** Once you've stated that the person's qualifications don't fit the position, don't describe the decision-making process or catalog a candidate's shortcomings. Elaborating increases the risk of offending the person or inadvertently running afoul of employment laws.

- **Don't give advice.** A rejection letter is the wrong venue for critiquing interview skills or providing tips on career-building. You don't want to put anything in writing that suggests the pathway to a future interview.

- **Avoid empty promises.** Don't say you'll keep the person in mind, or invite the candidate to keep in touch, unless you really mean it. But nothing is forever. The applicant you reject this month could be qualified for a position next month, so don't use language that writes off a candidate's future prospects. Keep the wording focused on the present hiring decision.

- **No jokes, nothing too personal.** To use the words of Michael Corleone from *The Godfather*, a rejection letter is "strictly business."

- **No drama, either.** It's tough to be a hiring manager. Share your anguish with colleagues, not applicants. Lamenting how difficult it was to choose the other finalist isn't useful.

A much better example:

Dear Samantha,

Thank you for applying for the position of sales representative with QRS Corp. I appreciated the chance to discuss the scope of the job and learn more about your career goals during our recent Zoom conversation. Unfortunately, we aren't able to offer you the position. Other candidates under consideration have stronger experience related to the responsibilities we envision.

Wishing you much success in your future endeavors,

Joan Foster
Regional Sales Manager, QRS Corp

A rejection letter isn't an exercise in creativity. Keep it unexciting. The safest ground is well trod.

Boost Your Résumé

Assuming you already have the basics, below are tips to spice things up:

- **Keep it to a single page.** People are more likely to read it, and the space limitation will force you to share only what's relevant to the employer. You'll be forced to justify every word.

- **Customize for the job.** A résumé isn't your autobiography. It should be a tailored timeline of experiences that have molded you to become the right person for this specific position. Include the experiences and skills that are pertinent to *this* role.

- **Cut the personality traits.** Here's a sample of the "Objective Statement" of a licensed esthetician: "I'm a hardworking, reliable, and focused individual who is always willing to go above and beyond to support and serve my clients." We hate to break it to you, but "hardworking" and "reliable" are basic requirements. Employers expect this. Cut the soft skills and use that precious real estate to share your technical skills.

- **Use data.** Here's a sample from a résumé of a restaurant manager: "Oversaw and managed the front-of-house team." Add numbers and you'll get: "Managed, trained, and scheduled more than seventy-five front-of-house staff members." Suddenly, we've revved up your management experience. We can now imagine the pace and the size of this restaurant, along with the responsibilities it required to keep the operation moving.

- **Highlight your impact.** Let's say you "revamped all dining room training programs." All right, how did that help the customer? Or the business? Like so: "Focused on staff education and upselling techniques to help increase check averages by 10 percent." Don't be shy now—this is the time to brag.

How to Pitch a Journalist Without Being Annoying

People email journalists when they want them to cover a story.

But journalists are inundated with story pitches. They receive dozens a week, most of them not newsworthy. You'll need a seriously effective pitch to get noticed.

First, ask yourself: Is your story new, radically unusual, or timely? If your answer is no, that is what we mean by an unworthy pitch, and this process should end here. But if you're sure the answer is yes, especially if it's yes to more than one of those, here's what to do:

- **Find the right journalist.** There are few things that annoy busy journalists more than getting emails that have nothing to do with their beat. Do enough research to make sure you're sending it to the right person in the newsroom. And it never hurts to let a reporter know you've read their work by saying something like, "Since you wrote that excellent story last month about Ariceli's Tacos, I thought you might be interested in this news about another great neighborhood restaurant."

- **Email first, don't call.** In your email, present yourself and your story in as few words as possible. Don't forget to add tantalizing bits of detail to make your pitch unforgettable.

- **Send your email before 9 a.m. or in the afternoon between 1 p.m. and 3 p.m.** After 3 p.m., journalists will be writing and editing their daily stories, and they will not read your email. It will be buried. (And don't bother sending it at all on a Friday.)

- **Follow up.** If you don't receive a response within forty-eight hours, follow up with a gentle reminder email. Still no response? Call the journalist's office telephone during regular work hours. If there's no answer, leave a short message. If that fails, move on. Time is short, and not taking no for an answer now may earn you a permanent place on their list of "no way in hell."

Here are examples of how not to do it. First, the mystery pitch:

One of my team members volunteers at the zoo and recently assisted in a very special event there. Interested? Contact me and I'll tell you more.

What a tease! It takes one second to close an email—and this one is getting closed.

Here's another example of what to avoid—the hard sell:

I'm offering you a story that you'd be foolish to ignore. One of my team members volunteers at the zoo and helped at the birth of a baby giraffe yesterday. Get back to me quickly if you'd like to interview her. She's a lot more quotable than the people you usually interview.

All journalists—well, nearly all journalists—are human beings with emotions. They appreciate positive approaches, not insults. Which means tone is important. You're offering them an opportunity, but you're also asking them to do you a favor.

The trick is to write the kind of email that intrigues journalists, that makes them envision a successful outcome. Be straightforward and informative. Here's a helpful, snappy pitch:

Hello,

I've noticed you often write about people who volunteer in the community. One of my team members, Sara Lopez, volunteers at the zoo and helped at the birth of a baby giraffe yesterday. Please let me know if you'd like to interview the giraffe midwife, who is also our head of HR.

Thank you,
Jaya Bell
CEO, Bell Accounting Services

Be sure to include the name of the potential interview subject. The journalist might know them, or they may wish to google the person to see if they're overexposed in the media already. Include cell phone numbers, too.

And notice how the pitch includes a phrase, "giraffe midwife," that summarizes the story in two words. Newspeople love that. It might just show up in a headline.

If you want to pitch a journalist, let us help. Send a message to Melissa or Jenn on LinkedIn and we'll give you a few tips for improvement. LinkedIn.com/company/m-harris-co

Don't Announce Your Announcement

When you feel ready to share something new with your audience—a product, a feature, a sale—don't announce the announcement. That means no mass emails that read like this:

- Stay tuned. We're releasing our mobile app in just ten days.
- Our Kickstarter project launches in one week!
- Get ready. Three hours until you can get tickets.

You aren't building excitement; you're spamming. And lowering your credibility. Very few companies can share empty bulletins like this without losing subscribers or followers. (Basically, Apple, Disney, and Taylor Swift can pull this off. Small businesses can't.)

Respect your audience's time, and reach out only when you have something for them to do:

- It's here! Download our mobile app for free.
- Our Kickstarter project is live.
- Grab tickets right now at this link.

If you don't have an action for your audience besides "wait," you're not ready to make an announcement.

How to Write (and Give) a Speech

A graduation speech isn't the same as a keynote at the International Conference on Aardvark Conservation. But almost any speech will be served by the following tips:

- **Know what you want your speech to do.** If you're not sure, talk it through with a friend. A clear title—say, "How to Write (and Give) a Speech"—will steer you.

- **Say it out loud as you write.** Remember that a speech, whether you're writing it for yourself or someone else, is meant to be spoken. And heard. Vary the length of your sentences. Make most of them short. Not too many numbers.

- **Divide your speech into sections.** There's a reason books are divided into chapters. Two reasons, really. Chapters help the writer break ideas into manageable portions. They also give the audience a sense of traveling toward a goal. In a speech, you don't have to enumerate the sections for your listeners. However, they will appreciate a hint about how long they have to sit before they can go to the bathroom: "Now, for our final ten minutes, I'll get into . . ."

- **To quote or not to quote?** A couple of quotable quotes can fortify your own thoughts. But don't overuse other people's words. If you do quote, make sure you attribute—correctly.

- **Humor helps.** But don't measure the success of your speech by how many laughs you get. A touching story is better than a parade of weak jokes.

- **It's OK to be personal.** A speech is rarely the place to bare your whole soul. But even if you're talking about aardvarks, people appreciate a personal anecdote or two, especially if you can connect your life to theirs.

- **Create rapport with the audience.** Look at them. If you're in a small or medium-sized room, make relaxed eye contact with individuals, just a few seconds per person. Ask them a question or two.

- **Slow down by using frequent pauses.** The pause builds suspense and lets your words sink in. Comprehension occurs in the pauses.

- **No need to memorize your speech.** But rehearse it. Record it. Listen to it. Know it well enough that your eyes aren't always glued to your script. Consider highlighting key words with a yellow marker so that if you lose your place the important ideas are easily visible.

- **End strong.** Repeat a major point or two. Consider a dash of poetry. Or issue a call to action.

Before you face the crowd, get calm. Take a few full breaths. Then go give that great speech you're going to sit down right now and write.

Writing Effective Personal Communications

Personal communication is just as important as business communication. Just because you're writing to friends and relatives doesn't mean you should loosen your standards. Imagine if people were as careful with their language at family dinner as they are during job interviews. Much less screaming.

Here's advice for writing with personality while avoiding drama.

How to Thank Someone

Do you send thank-you notes? If you don't like to write them, know that a thank-you note doesn't need to be long and flowery in order to be meaningful. Here's a format to follow.

In the first sentence, name what it is you're thankful for. Get as specific as you can.

Instead of "Thank you for the gift," you should say, "Thank you for the beautiful flower bouquet."

"Thank you for your hard work" is kind but less personal than "Thank you for dedicating hours to this project."

"Thanks for being there" is a lovely sentiment but made even more meaningful with details: "Thank you for taking me out to dinner when I needed a night out."

Then, write a sentence or two sharing what the gesture means to you. Make sure the word "I" or "me" appears in this part. And probably the word "feel," too.

- You made me feel very appreciated.
- I am incredibly lucky to have you on my creative team.
- I feel much better. Sharing a meal with you turned my whole day around!

Close with a final expression of gratitude before signing your name.

- All my thanks.
- Thanks again for thinking of me.
- I'm grateful for your mentorship.

Put it all together, and voila:

Marcos,

I owe you tremendous thanks for taking over that last-minute assignment last week. Because of you, I was able to truly relax on my trip. I'm grateful to have a generous colleague like you.

Most sincerely,
Keanu

How to Complain

If you're writing a complaint letter, you're likely pissed off. But you don't want to sound that way in your letter. Reasonable people respond reasonably to other reasonable people.

Here's how to be reasonable:

- **Have all the details: dates, people you talked to, etc.** If you don't have that info, even a well-written complaint letter may be ineffective. Whenever you get on the phone with someone to resolve a problem, take notes that include the date, the name of the person you talked to, and what they said.

- **Write an opening sentence that states the problem in a measured, calm manner.** Be a grown-up. No tantrums.

- **It may not matter to customer service people, but you can add that you're a longtime customer (if you are).**

- **If you're sending an email, write a straightforward subject line that will get your message routed properly.**

- **Keep your note short.** People ignore long letters.

- **Don't include anything irrelevant, such as saying that this problem occurred just as you were trying to take your cat to the vet or that your birthday is coming up.**

- **State very explicitly what compensation you're demanding.** But don't use the word "demand."

Here's an example:

Subject line: Need refund for disrupted service in Evanston 4/5/24

Dear customer service rep,

I'm a longtime customer of your cable TV service, and I'm writing about a service disruption that affects my billing for April 2024.

At about 9 a.m. on April 5, 2024, my cable went out. I later found out that your company had mistakenly canceled my service when you meant to cancel a neighbor's.

At 10 a.m., I called your company and talked to a person named Richard who told me he expected my cable to be restored by noon. But service didn't return until 9 p.m. I'm requesting a full day's credit on my bill.

Please respond by phone or email to confirm that a day's service will be removed from my bill immediately.

Thank you.

The best four words to describe an effective complaint letter: polite, brief, firm, and factual.

How to Write a Sympathy Note

When the loved one of someone you know dies, it's hard to know what to say. Most people are afraid to say something wrong, so they say nothing at all.

But you're writing, not talking, so you have time to gather your thoughts, and there's less of a chance you'll say something you'll regret.

The formula for a good sympathy note, if you know the person who died, is simple: Tell them you're sorry for their loss. Recall a positive memory. Restate your condolences.

> Dear Camille,
> I was so sorry to hear that you lost your sister, Mary. She was my favorite babysitter growing up. She taught me how to play chess during all those afternoons after school. My condolences to you and your family.
> —Your Name

That's it. Simple and brief. Write your note in a sympathy card or in a blank card with an understated image on the front. Then mail it.

If you didn't know the deceased, try something more general:

> Dear Joan,
> I was so sorry to hear that you lost your father. His obituary was beautiful. I found his lifelong dedication to animal rights inspirational. My condolences to you and your whole family.
> —Your Name

Things to avoid:

- Don't bring religion or a deity into it. Not everyone is comforted by "God's plan."
- Even if you know that the person was sick for a long time, don't say that they're in a better place. Leave out judgments like "It's for the best," unless you want to get smacked in the face.
- Don't assume the dynamics of their relationship, like that they were on good terms.
- Don't try to be funny. Share a happy memory if you have one, but no comedy.

A well-done sympathy card lets the living know that you care—and that their loved one deserved a pause and a pen to paper.

How to Get Guests to Actually RSVP

If you're planning an event that requires extra prep work—buying food, buying tickets, booking a venue—it's appropriate to require an RSVP. Here's how to write it so people actually respond.

> Are you attending, and are you bringing a guest? Let me know by Oct. 22 so I can arrange enough food for everybody!
>
> Please note: I need to reserve our seats, so please RSVP by this Friday. Thank you!

Tell your guests *when* you need an RSVP and *why*. Explain the reasoning—the consequences. That will, hopefully, do the trick to get you what you need. If it doesn't, issue a reminder to the unresponsive guests all at once. Keep your note polite but short and specific:

> Hello, all! Will we see you at our wedding? Our caterer needs an accurate head count, so please RSVP by June 18. Take care!

Don't include other details in this message. It's RSVP time. Anything else will muck up your message.

For the last one or two particularly stubborn stragglers, send a direct, personal note straight to them:

> Hi, friend! Are you attending our wedding on July 13? Hope you can—please just let us know.

And if that fails? The problem clearly isn't in your writing. Unfortunately, it's time to call.

How to Write a Toast Without Embarrassing Anyone

Oh God. Oh no. It's happening. You've been asked to give a toast to the lucky couple.

The good part about toasts is that no one is going to remember much of what you say.

Unless, of course, you say something really stupid.

Here are tips to avoid disaster:

- **Rehearse out loud.** Yes, that means you're going to need to write it all out ahead of time. This will help you avoid going down blind alleys. If you start to ramble, you're in trouble. Know your speech well enough that you can give most or all of it without referring to your printout. (But have the printout handy just in case.)

- **Be loud and clear.** Wedding receptions happen in big halls with tables spread out, and some guests may be hard of hearing. Make sure your microphone works. Speak slowly. Over-enunciate. And recruit a friend to stand at the back of the venue and signal you if you need to speak louder.

- **Be punchy.** Keep sentences short and emphasize the most important words, the way TV news anchors do.

- **Be brief.** Have you ever heard people complaining that a wedding toast was too short? We haven't.

- **Tell a funny story, but don't embarrass anyone.** Pick a single point or theme you want to emphasize. (My friend is loyal, the couple is a perfect match, etc.) Make sure your anecdotes demonstrate your point instead of distracting from it.

- **Avoid anecdotes involving drugs and alcohol.** That story about your buddy throwing furniture out the window of his fraternity house will upset Meemaw.

- **No inside jokes.** Remember your audience. Distant relatives and not-so-close friends also attend wedding receptions. Making inside jokes shuts them out.

- **In the end, be sincere.** You may have an irreverent relationship with the spouse who is your pal, but sarcasm and insults don't play well, especially to close. Finish your toast with a sincere sentiment that everyone can happily toast.

- **If you plan to have a drink, do it afterward.** You may think you'll be less nervous if you down three or four beers before your toast. But, in fact, you'll be slurry, unfocused, and more likely to say the wrong thing.

- **Get the names right.** This may seem obvious, but here's a story. A young man's marriage ended, he divorced the woman, and he married another woman. The man's friend gave a toast at the second wedding, ending the speech with "And now, let's toast Oscar and Martha." Problem was, Oscar had just married Amelia. Martha was the name of the first wife. This is why we say you should have a few drinks—afterward. And it's why your goal shouldn't be to give the perfect toast. Your goal should be to make your toast a pleasant but forgettable part of a happy event. Don't make a lasting bad impression on Martha. Um, Amelia.

Here's a sample toast that can get you started:

My name is Danny Lopez. I was Dontae's college roommate, so we've had a lot of good times together—like the time [short story that is not weird or humiliating and does not involve throwing furniture out a window].

Something changed our senior year: Dontae was suddenly spending a lot less time around our apartment. I come to find out, it's because he's met someone. Someone special. Now, it took a few weeks of prodding, but Dontae finally let me meet this mystery man.

The second I met Caleb, I understood why I wasn't seeing my roommate as often: because he'd found the love of his life.

Today, I'm tremendously lucky to call them both my dear friends. Caleb is [insert a few genuine compliments about Caleb].

I am overjoyed for these two. So please, everyone, let's raise a toast to the newlyweds.

How to Write a Holiday Letter People Will Enjoy Reading

The annual holiday letter is an opportunity to share what's going on with you or your family. Not everyone does this—some people just send polite greetings, or don't send cards at all—but if you like providing a yearly update about your life, here's how to do it.

The trick: Limit yourself. Create a framework that constrains your space or comes with its own template. You'll be surprised how freeing this limitation actually is. You no longer have to be complete or definitive.

Idea No. 1: Let the calendar be your guide with a month-by-month breakdown. This doesn't require a good memory; your smartphone's photo library has been keeping visual notes for you. Plus, you just need one item per month; this is a holiday letter, not a full report.

January:	Shockingly little snow! Didn't matter as Judy was recovering from knee replacement surgery.
February:	Celebrated Valentine's Day at home. See January.
March:	John started *Game of Thrones* and got nothing else done.
April:	Malcolm got his driver's license! Oh God.

Idea No. 2: Allot one paragraph or long sentence of space to each family member and abandon prose for a quick list.

John:	Rebuilt the back deck, hated every second of it, and vows never to do it again.

Judy: Planted a new garden with enough vegetables to supply the whole neighborhood. Move over, Martha Stewart.

Emma: Fell in love with softball and proved to be an incredible athlete, inspiring neighbors to wonder if she was adopted.

Orzo & Panini: Are dogs, so they did cute dog stuff.

Malcolm: Got his driver's license in April, against our better judgment.

Idea No. 3: Let the holiday season guide you, be it the seven days of Kwanzaa, the eight days of Hanukkah, or the twelve days of Christmas. They might start like this:

Happy holidays! We hope your new year is joyous!
Here's our year by the numbers:

ONE single athlete in the entire family now that Emma has fallen in love with softball

TWO dogs in the house now that we've adopted Orzo

THREE gazillion trips to the hardware store before John completed the new back deck. (Pro tip: Hire a contractor.)

FOUR drivers in the family now that Malcolm got his driver's license in April, terrifying all of us

Idea No. 4: If you want to keep it real, share your highs and lows from the year. This idea can be used to further refine many of the previous examples.

**Happy holidays! We hope your new year includes
more highlights and fewer lowlights!**

OUR HIGHLIGHTS (hurray!)

- We bought a new car, a Honda CR-V, and really like it.
- Emma hit two home runs in the first round of the state softball tournament.
- John completed the new back deck. (And even better news: Next time he promises to hire a contractor.)
- Malcolm got his driver's license in April.
- Judy got her knee replaced in January, and she's already outracing the rest of the family.

OUR LOWLIGHTS (boo!)

- Our 2012 Toyota Sienna gave up the ghost on the Kennedy Expressway (which is why we bought a new Honda CR-V).
- Emma's team lost in the first round of the state softball tournament (despite her two home runs).
- John mismeasured the wood for the back deck and we had to buy new lumber (but John has now developed a deeper relationship with the tape measure).
- Two weeks after getting his driver's license, Malcolm ran into a pole in the Walmart parking lot. (But no one was hurt.)

OUR BOTTOM LINE
**We're all still here, and that's a victory.
Love to all our family and friends.**

Idea No. 5: Lean into your passions. Instead of sharing what each family member did, list their favorite books or songs or movies—or all three! Your friends can learn a lot about who you are from this information, and you have the joy of sharing what brought you enjoyment through the year.

Happy holidays! Here's what we loved this year.

EMMA

Movie/TV: *Queen Charlotte: A Bridgerton Story*

Song: "I Can See You (Taylor's Version)" by Taylor Swift

Book: *Lessons in Chemistry* by Bonnie Garmus

JOHN

Movie/TV: *Asteroid City*

Song: "Tangled Up in Blue" by Bob Dylan (sorry, I'm not up on today's music)

Book: *Crook Manifesto* by Colson Whitehead

MALCOLM

Movie/TV: *Guardians of the Galaxy Vol. 3*

Song: "Waffle House" by Jonas Brothers

Book: *Killers of the Flower Moon* by David Grann

JUDY

Movie/TV: *Only Murders in the Building*

Song: "We Didn't Start the Fire" by Fall Out Boy

Book: *The Lincoln Highway* by Amor Towles

But our favorite entertainment is seeing our family and friends. Don't be a stranger in the new year!

If all this seems excessive, that's because it is. But the people who rarely see you will enjoy a look into your year. This is the one time we'll encourage you to write *more*.

What to Write to Someone Who Ghosted You (Professionally, Romantically, or Both)

Everything seemed so promising. You hit it off, had a great convo over coffee, and agreed to hang out again. Since then? Crickets. Your texts go unanswered. Your calls go to voicemail.

You conjure up all sorts of excuses, but you know the truth: You've been ghosted.

You want an explanation. You deserve an explanation. You're going to demand an explanation. Let us help.

First, summon the full breadth of your fiery rage.

Next, start typing. Type without mercy.

Explain how hurtful it is to be rejected in this way, with no warning or closure; point out that you have many other attractive and dependable options; make clear that you deserve an apology but do not expect and would not accept one from such a heartless coward; and forbid them from attempting to contact you ever again.

Finish with a dismissive *enjoy the rest of your life.*

And then delete everything you just wrote. Block them if you want.

And enjoy the rest of your life.

A Few More Tips
for Any Kind of Writing

Quality writing matters, whether it's a note to your neighbor complaining about their yappy dog or a proposal to win a $10 million contract. Here are a few more things to keep in mind.

Keep to One Idea per Sentence

If you're writing something dense that has many branches (academics and scientists, listen up), here's a trick: Limit yourself to one idea per sentence. Just one. Take this unwieldy example:

> Sometimes, financial barriers may not originate from formal regulatory issues but may instead come from the surrounding public perceptions or social license to operate.

And dice it into:

> Financial barriers may not originate from formal regulatory issues. Instead, they could stem from public perceptions or the social license to operate.

Humans have terrible reading comprehension. Every time you slice a long sentence, you're doing your readers a favor.

Handle Quotes Like a Pro

Using quotes boosts the quality of your writing. Quotes evoke the human voice, which carries more weight than regular text. Consider these tips to ensure they are as effective as they can be:

- **Use quotes that deliver impactful news, use entertaining language, or reveal emotion.** If the quote offers none of the above, you likely can do better paraphrasing. Imagine interviewing your CEO and her saying, "We are pleased by the long-term prospects of our product pipeline and believe that our market metrics will bear out that optimism." Businesslike. And boring. Especially considering that ten minutes earlier she had said, "Once the public sees what this product can do, we won't be able to keep it on the shelves." Paraphrase the first; quote the second.

- **Identify the speaker as early as possible.** This usually means after the first sentence, though it can follow a natural pause.

  - **Preferred:**
    "Don't write so that you can be understood, write so that you can't be misunderstood," said William Howard Taft.

  - **Also OK:**
    "Don't write so that you can be understood," said William Howard Taft, "write so that you can't be misunderstood." (Notice this still is one sentence: comma after the attribution and the continuation begins with a lowercase letter.)

- **Don't use quote marks for emphasis.** Air quotes don't translate well to the printed page. Trying to indicate sarcasm or show doubt using quotes is easily misunderstood. Let the words deliver that information. A recent example:

> False claims that the 2020 election was "stolen" are fueling backlash and intimidation campaigns across the country.

The quotes around "stolen" above aren't needed; the sentence clearly states the claims are false. And consider this example:

> Acme Products CEO John James said it was a "safe" product.

We read this as the writer not-so-slyly indicating disbelief. But could it mean the exact opposite? Is the writer emphasizing that the product is safe? Confusion reigns.

- **"Said" is enough.** Let the quote do the talking and keep the attribution simple. If the speaker laughed, scowled, proclaimed, or tittered, it should be clear in the words themselves. If you feel compelled to point it out, do it elsewhere. The one exception: "asked."

- **Commas and periods go inside the quote marks.** The meaning of the sentence will decide where semicolons, colons, and question marks fall. The exclamation mark? If you have to use one—and you don't—it follows the rule for question marks.

- **Be judicious.** The power of quoted material wanes with every added sentence. More than one paragraph of quoted material not only loses its punch, most readers will skip it. If you need to cite large globs of text, consider additional typographical treatments, such as indenting the section or italicizing it. Also, know that there are rule quirks when punctuating multiple paragraphs of quoted material. The easiest way to deal with that is to not quote anything longer than two or three sentences.

Be Vivid

Humans love images. It's scientific: Our brains absorb visuals faster than words. It's why we advocate for using photography and art whenever possible. But when you can't, at least use vivid words. Like so:

- "It's humid outside" changes to "The air feels like clam chowder."
- "It stormed loudly" changes to "Rain pummeled the windows."
- "I'm busy and tired" becomes "This week flattened me to the floor."

- "We'll make your writing stronger" becomes "We'll refine your writing to a razor-sharp point."

When you read something that evokes the senses, your brain responds. Your sensory cortex lights up. The more your writing evokes sounds, smells, and textures, the more you've engaged your reader.

Go Long, Then Go Short

Think of the last time you danced at a wedding. Maybe you're trying to forget that moment, but too bad. What was it that made you jump up to dance? (Besides peer pressure.)

It was the playlist. The best, most memorable playlists offer variability: some pop, some rock, that one Journey song toward the end of the night. It's the DJ's job to build in a few surprises.

As a writer, your job is not much different. To keep your audience engaged, vary the length of your sentences.

Read this:

> In an effort to reduce the effects of climate change, more and more farmers are using "regenerative farming" techniques. One example of regenerative farming is adopting a "no-tillage" policy. Tillage is the practice of frequently overturning soil, which can make the soil lose nutrients and render it useless for growth.

Now read our rewrite:

> To reduce the effects of climate change, more farmers are using "regenerative farming" techniques. One such technique: a "no-tillage" policy. Tillage is the practice of frequently overturning soil—which can destroy its nutrients. And soil without nutrients is useless.

See what we did? We went back and forth with long and short sentences to keep our guests on the dance floor.

Choose Precisely the Right Word

A single word can energize a tired sentence. But too many writers allow their sentences to sit there dull and unadorned, like a row of garbage cans on a curbside.

Here are our tips on word choice:

- **Know what you overuse.** Every writer has phrases they grab for over and over again. Figure out what yours are, do a word search for them after you finish writing, and replace them with synonyms as appropriate. (Words we chronically overuse and had to cut from this book: "showcase," "critical," and "compelling.")

- **Don't be so damn ordinary.** Among the words that make your sentences feel bland: "good," "bad," "big," "little," "lots," "great," "happy," "sad," "nice," "like," "really," "very," "important," and "interesting." Interestingly enough, the word "interesting" isn't very interesting.

- **Consult a thesaurus.** This is not cheating—it's what professionals do. But don't assume every word offered will work equally well, and don't pick the fanciest, most complicated word on the list. Don't use "pontificate" when you could use "lecture." And don't use "lecture" when you could use "say."

- **Don't use ridiculous synonyms.** If you're writing about snow, it's OK to call it "snow" over and over. In badly written news stories, you'll sometimes see snow described as "the white stuff" because someone once told a writer to do that. Don't do that.

- **Don't let a single word derail you.** If you're struggling over a word choice but are otherwise enjoying strong writing momentum, put XXXX in your sentence where you know you'll need the word, and keep typing away. Go back later and fill in the right word. (Don't forget that part.)

- **Be a logophile and build your vocabulary.** That means "a lover of words," for those of us who haven't taken the SAT in a few decades.

Get Active

Writing coaches pound on the idea that sentences should be active, not passive. It's one of the easiest ways to resurrect a lifeless sentence.

Active voice also makes your sentences more understandable. Readers expect the main actor in a sentence to come first. Then they want the verb to follow and tell them what that actor is doing. It's just logical.

Passive voice often leads to bad writing because it obscures who is doing what.

Here's a sports headline:

Jerry Jones: Every opportunity was given for the Rams to remain in St. Louis

Jones didn't say who provided the opportunity, so perhaps the headline writers were stuck with the passive construction. But the headline created confusion about whether Jones thought the football team or the city wasted the opportunity. It reeks of avoidance.

Naturally, politicians love this. When they say "mistakes were made," they hope no one asks who made those mistakes.

A headline on an Oregon TV station website read:

Portland mayor admits mistakes were made in police response to brawls in Northeast Portland, downtown

In the story, Mayor Ted Wheeler said: "I take full responsibility for it." So why didn't the news story let him fully own it? Clearly, in that news report, mistakes were made.

Don't Fumble the Handoff

One of the most difficult challenges for writers is to make sentences work together so there's a sense of continuity. When it's not clear why one sentence follows another, it's a speed bump that wrecks your reader's momentum.

Let's look at these two sentences:

> The school's chemistry teacher also works as a dance instructor at a local studio. A principal in a nearby town has a part-time job as night manager of a Chipotle, and also sells insurance.

They're two sentences that happen to be in the same paragraph. Let's make them work together:

> The school's chemistry teacher also works as a dance instructor at a local studio. Such moonlighting is increasingly necessary because of this state's low education salaries. A principal in a nearby town has it even harder. He has two additional jobs: as an insurance salesman and night manager of a Chipotle.

See? We didn't just give the reader two statements of fact. We put the facts in alliance and explained their significance.

Here's another example of two sentences that need to be sewn together more effectively:

Dissatisfaction among the supermarket's staff has led to a high rate of absenteeism. The store manager says customers are complaining that store shelves are empty while there's plenty of stock in the back.

Here's one way to fix it:

Dissatisfaction among the supermarket's staff has led to a high rate of absenteeism. That has led, in turn, to empty store shelves even though there's plenty of stock in the back.

And here's an even simpler edit:

Dissatisfaction among the supermarket's staff has led to a high rate of absenteeism, leaving store shelves unfilled even though there's plenty of stock in back.

Don't Trip over Transitions

Just as it's vital for your sentences to work together, it's crucial to stitch together different sections of the same piece of writing with smooth transitions. Here's an example.

> . . . and that's how Abe Saperstein made the Harlem Globetrotters a national basketball sensation.
>
> Saperstein's interest in Negro Leagues baseball allowed him to arrange frequent non-league barnstorming tours that boosted the players' pay.

Wait a second. You were talking about basketball. Now you're talking about baseball. Is this a new section? Let's make that clear:

> . . . and that's how Abe Saperstein made the Harlem Globetrotters a national basketball sensation.
>
> Baseball also was high on Saperstein's agenda. He leveraged the contacts he'd made through basketball to set up baseball barnstorming tours that brought extra money to Negro Leagues players when they weren't playing league games.

You've clearly signaled the start of a new section, and you've demonstrated why it's logical that you wrote about Saperstein's baseball work after you described his basketball work. It's like you actually planned it that way, because you did.

One more note: If you're struggling to make two sentences or two sections of text work in tandem, it might not mean you're a lousy wordsmith. It might mean you're struggling to write a logical transition because your sentences or sections of text are in the wrong place or in the wrong order. Consider reorganizing.

Add Value by Subtraction

We'll close here with the 20-Word Challenge. Right before you hit send or publish your next piece, cut twenty words.

Fewer words, more value

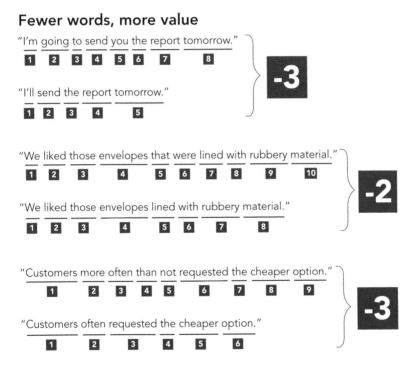

Note that the meaning didn't change one bit. Sentences that sounded academic and stuffy became more conversational. Plus, you saved the reader's time.

We like what essayist Paul Graham has to say about this: "The easier something is to read, the more deeply readers will engage with it. The less energy they expend on your prose, the more they'll have left for your ideas."

Using Artificial Intelligence Intelligently

We couldn't, in good conscience, publish a writing advice book without including a section on generative artificial intelligence (AI).

McKinsey & Company defines it well: "Algorithms (such as ChatGPT) that can be used to create new content, including audio, code, images, text, simulations, and videos."

But this field of AI is advancing faster than we can advise on it, at least in a book. What we've attempted here is to offer foundational guidance we think will endure for years.

If it doesn't, we'll simply sell updated editions, and you'll have to keep buying it forever.

Hang On, Don't Be Gross About This

AI *can* improve your writing. Think of it as a tool, like spell-check: It should be used in conjunction with human judgment and expertise. AI can't replace your own creativity, emotion, originality, and lived experience. So don't use it when you're writing:

- **Commentary, opinions, and personal essays, especially ones used for college admissions.** A column, op-ed, or personal essay is the epitome of the expression of your voice and perspective—meaning AI should be far away. You *can* use it as a resource to summarize or contextualize background information on your topic (more on this later).

- **Eulogies and other tributes.** A eulogy is a personal tribute, so tasking a machine with this feels gross, doesn't it? AI has the word "artificial" right in the name. You don't want to write an artificial memorial in someone's honor. The same concept applies to toasts and other commendations. AI can provide you a framework to follow—much like Google can, only better—but write from your experience.

- **Reporting and prose.** This includes journalism, fiction, and poetry. Anything that will appear under your byline should be yours and yours alone.

- **Resignations.** Don't let AI write your resignation letter or help you with your breakup speech—but do use it to prepare for hard conversations by anticipating potential responses or objections and even as an interactive partner for rehearsing (more on this later, too).

We do recommend using AI to help you write:

- **Cover letters and applications.** Best practice is, of course, to write a custom cover letter for each position you apply for. But this sucks. It's time-consuming. Job hunting is hard enough as it is. Let the robots help with outlines and ideas—like a list of relevant job skills. Don't use it to lie about yourself; use it to highlight what you're best at. Then you can refine its output by adding more context or information. Rewrite it to bring in more nuance and ensure it's in your voice—and always edit and proofread carefully before submitting.

- **Google ads.** AI can simplify some of the time-consuming tasks in setting up pay-per-click campaigns, like doing keyword research and even generating ad headlines. You can also ask AI to iterate or shift tone of voice for the copy you like best.

- **Job descriptions.** These should be clean and descriptive, and they should motivate people to apply. Provide AI with a list of qualities and experiences you're looking for and a description of the job. The tool can clean it up for you and suggest additions based on industry best practices. Be sure to review and edit for voice.

- **User manuals.** ChatGPT can be used as a tool for user manuals and instructional materials by easily generating informative text based on provided information. With specific, relevant input, AI can make the copywriting more relatable, and easy to follow. Make sure your engineer or product designer checks it.

This list isn't exhaustive, and some assignments will take you into gray areas that have you looking longingly at ChatGPT. Before you use it, ask yourself: *Is this content personal? Will it be attributed to me? Is it grounded in my point of view? Will it be graded, judged, or rewarded?*

If the answer is yes, don't use AI. Write it yourself.

Rehearse Tough Conversations

If you're due for an uncomfortable conversation with a colleague, jot down your talking points first. Imagine their responses, and how you'll react. Practice the worst-case scenario, but imagine the conversation going really well, too.

This is a meaningful exercise because when the time comes to talk, you'll (hopefully) have a strong command of your emotions. AI can help by providing a sample conversation.

Here's our prompt: *Practice a tough conversation in which I have to ask someone why they're not meeting their deadlines.*

Here's what we got back:

> **You:** Hi, [Colleague's Name], can I speak with you for a moment?
>
> **Colleague:** Sure, what's up?
>
> **You:** I wanted to talk to you about the recent missed deadlines. I've noticed that you haven't been able to meet some of the project timelines we discussed. It's become a concern for the team, and I wanted to understand what's been going on.
>
> **Colleague:** Oh, well, I've been dealing with some personal issues lately, and it's been affecting my ability to focus on work. I'm sorry about the delays.
>
> **You:** I understand that personal issues can arise, and I empathize with your situation. However, it's important that we address this as it affects the

team's productivity and the overall success of
the project. Is there anything specific that's been
causing these delays?

Hmm. Strong opener, but let's hit pause. If your colleague says, "I've been dealing with some personal issues lately," that could mean anything from a death in the family to a faulty Wi-Fi connection. AI doesn't understand human emotion (yet).

And, sure, your colleague should have clued you in earlier that they need some work reassigned. But that's in the past, and humans are going to be humans. So do better than AI and speak like one, because the phrase "I empathize with your situation" is not empathetic. Here's how to be both constructive and kind:

- I'm sorry to hear that. Let's come up with some ways to make this easier on you and the team.
- Thank you for sharing that.
- How can we best support you right now?

Putting professional words to conflicting emotions is difficult, and AI can get you started with a rough draft. But then it's your responsibility to edit it.

Or just give up and ask the robot to try again.

Like so: *Practice a tough conversation in which I have to ask someone why they're not meeting their deadlines and I am empathetic.*

You: Hi, [Colleague's Name], can we have a moment to talk?

Colleague: Of course, what's on your mind?

You: I wanted to have a conversation about the recent missed deadlines. I've noticed that you've been struggling to meet some of the project timelines we established. I wanted to understand what might be causing this and offer my support, if needed.

Colleague: I appreciate your concern. To be honest, I've been facing some challenges recently that have made it difficult to meet the deadlines. I've been feeling overwhelmed and finding it hard to concentrate.

You: Thank you for sharing that with me. It takes courage to open up about difficulties. I want you to know that I'm here to support you, both professionally and personally.

Now that warmed our cold, dead hearts.

Get Unstuck

Every writer gets stuck. Sometimes it's for a scary reason, like an overwhelming hundred-page assignment. Sometimes it's over routine snags, like finding the right transition. It's frustrating—and can be panic-inducing if you're on deadline.

AI can be your not-so-secret weapon for:

- **Brainstorming.** AI can be the spark you need when you're low on creativity and momentum. You can use it to brainstorm:
  - Titles and summaries for novels, short stories, TV series, podcasts, etc.
  - World-building and character development in fiction writing
  - Article and white paper topics

- **Giving you an opener.** We've all experienced the tyranny of the blank page—but AI can help you escape it. Think of it as another colleague to bounce ideas off, because even bad ideas give you something to react to.

  Keep in mind that you'll want to feed it the same backstory you'd feed a colleague. Provide context so it knows what you're writing about. Include keywords if relevant to the assignment. Give examples of voice and tone—both what you're looking for and what to avoid.

- **Finding alternative words.** When the word you're looking for is on the tip of your tongue but you just can't find it, AI can help—faster than a thesaurus or even the wittiest word wizard. You can plug a sentence or a paragraph into the tool and ask it for alternative nouns or verbs. Its suggestions might be just what you're looking for—or perhaps even something better.

- **Suggesting transitions.** Tap AI for ideas on a word, phrase, or even a paragraph to help connect one section to the next. You might end up with a cliché, but it can help get your momentum restarted.

- **Providing feedback.** AI can strengthen your writing or the structure of your piece when you ask it for feedback on grammar, sentence structure, tone, and flow. It's particularly helpful when you're so close to your writing that it's difficult to know where to focus to improve it. Start by sharing your draft. Include your intended audience, context, and desired tone of voice or style for more specific, targeted output.

What you get out of it is only as good as what you put in, so be specific in both your initial requests and subsequent refinements.

Study Up

It takes thirty minutes of concentrating for a human to read an in-depth magazine article. It takes AI seconds to spit out a detailed summary. The speed of AI gives us silly mortals the opportunity to absorb more new information and learn complex topics at a faster pace.

But you still need to do the thinking for yourself. Chatbots have tons of computing power, but not reasoning skill (yet).

So why use the bot? Instant education.

Let's say you want to understand why certain nations dominate semiconductor manufacturing. A Google search identifies a *Wired* magazine cover story, "I Saw the Face of God in a Semiconductor Factory," by Virginia Heffernan. Give that information to the chatbot and ask for five main points. You'll get an instantaneous overview.

Not detailed enough? Ask for five more highlights, then follow up further: Does the article *say* anything specific? You'll get answers from the bot.

Just don't expect it to do all your work. ChatGPT will summarize articles or books—anything available on the web within the chatbot's reach. You still need to fact-check. (Also, don't share the summary as your own work.)

Further, the bot's answers are precise but stiff. You can ask for a summary of the lovely 1960 *New Yorker* article by John Updike about baseball legend Ted Williams, but you'll only get a feel for Williams's hitting and Updike's writing by reading it. The bot knows about poetry; it doesn't appreciate poetry.

There's one more limitation: access. Chatbots can't always retrieve copyrighted material. But there are workarounds.

If you're interested in free-market economics and ask ChatGPT to summarize a famous 1973 *Playboy* magazine interview with economist Milton Friedman, the chatbot might decline because it's copyrighted.

To get around this specific copyright issue, we typed a reminder to the chatbot that Friedman's interview was widely read and deeply influential. "What did people think about the article?" we asked. This prompted the bot to provide "some general insights" about public reception to the article. Good stuff. Re-asking the question in a slightly different manner often nudges the bot to go deeper on a subject.

The more you prod, the more you'll get. And you can't annoy ChatGPT, so you might as well keep poking.

Get Organized

Outlines are essential in structuring content, creating a narrative arc, and ensuring a piece hits all the key points. They take time and thought, so of course everyone hates doing them.

This is where AI can be your champion. Provide it with your topic or idea, and it can punch out themes, related concepts, and subtopics, organized in a logical way.

We started with clear instructions: "Hello, bionic overlord. Can you please give me an outline for a report on the future uses of nuclear energy inside homes?"

ChatGPT not only supplied an outline; it added a good title and decent abstract. What a show-off. Here are the results.

Energizing Homes of Tomorrow: Unlocking the Potential of Residential Nuclear Energy

This white paper explores the transformative potential of integrating nuclear energy into residential settings. Advancements in small modular reactors (SMRs), microreactors, and nuclear battery technologies have opened up new possibilities for nuclear energy within homes. This paper discusses the advantages, challenges, and policy implications associated with residential nuclear energy, considering its potential to enhance energy security, reduce emissions, and provide reliable power.

The paper provides an overview of nuclear energy, its historical context, and current applications. It then delves into future prospects, including advanced SMRs, microreactors, hybrid systems, and the use of nuclear energy for water purification and residential heating. Safety considerations, waste management, and public perception are examined, alongside policy recommendations for safe implementation. By exploring the potential of residential nuclear energy, this white paper aims to foster informed discussions and contribute to decision-making regarding the future of residential power generation.

1. Introduction
    - Background and motivation
    - Purpose and scope of the white paper

2. Small Modular Reactors (SMRs)
    - Overview of SMRs and their characteristics
    - Benefits of SMRs for residential applications
    - Safety features and regulatory considerations
    - Potential challenges and solutions

3. Microreactors
    - Introduction to microreactor technology
    - Advantages of microreactors in residential settings
    - Design considerations and scalability
    - Safety features and risk mitigation

4. Residential Nuclear Energy Applications
    - Electricity generation and grid independence
    - District heating and cooling
    - Hydrogen production for clean fuel
    - Desalination for water scarcity regions
    - Industrial processes and waste management

5. Safety and Regulatory Framework
   - Safety considerations for residential nuclear energy
   - Licensing and regulatory challenges
   - Emergency preparedness and response
   - Public perception and education

6. Economic Viability and Affordability
   - Cost analysis of residential nuclear energy systems
   - Comparison with alternative energy sources
   - Long-term economic benefits and potential savings

7. Environmental Impact
   - Greenhouse gas emissions reduction potential
   - Waste management and disposal strategies
   - Life cycle analysis and sustainability considerations

8. Public Perception and Social Acceptance
   - Public attitudes toward residential nuclear energy
   - Communication and transparency in decision-making
   - Community engagement and acceptance strategies

9. Case Studies and Pilot Projects
   - Overview of existing residential nuclear energy projects
   - Lessons learned and best practices
   - Future prospects and potential deployment scenarios

10. Conclusion
    - Summary of key findings
    - Recommendations for further research and development
    - Concluding thoughts on the future of nuclear energy in homes

11. References
    • Citations for all sources used in the white paper

Your outline will not be perfect on the first attempt. In this case, ChatGPT's outline for the introduction looked long and impressive, but it was actually quite pitiful. We prompted next, "Now, please make the outline of the introduction more detailed and less generic."

1. Introduction
    • Background: Discuss the increasing global demand for clean and sustainable energy sources, along with the challenges posed by climate change and the need to reduce greenhouse gas emissions. Highlight the role of nuclear energy in providing a low-carbon alternative to fossil fuels.
    • Motivation: Explain the need to explore the potential of nuclear energy within residential settings as a means to promote energy efficiency, reduce reliance on traditional grid systems, and address energy poverty in remote or underdeveloped regions.
    • Research objective: Clearly state the purpose of the white paper, which is to examine the feasibility, benefits, challenges, and potential applications of nuclear energy systems within homes.

Ask for even more. If you need more specific details within the outline, you can ask ChatGPT to expand on certain sections or provide additional subtopics: "More on the advantages of microreactors in homes, please."

Even ChatGPT knows, though, that you can't use an app to sub-stitute for using your own brain. We close this chapter with some wise parting words from the chatbot itself:

> Remember that ChatGPT's suggestions are based on patterns it has learned from a vast amount of training data. It can pro-vide you with inspiration, ideas, and a starting point for your outline, but it's essential to review and customize the output to fit your specific needs and style.

Yes. We couldn't have said it better ourselves. (Wait. Uh-oh . . .)

Chapter 2

Let's Top It

To whom it may concern,

Hello there! We hope this email finds you well and that you're doing great and we hope you had a great weekend and that your week is off to a great start. Have a Happy Monday and a Happy Hump Day and a Happy Friday and hope you had a great weekend and a great vacation and a great life and we'll see you Monday.

We call these openers "throat clearers." They're not great.

In this section, we'll show you how to top your writing so your audience will want to read on instead of smash their phone with a hammer.

Getting Opened

Nail the First Line in a Business Email

The first sentence of your email is your first impression. It's a promise that your message is worth the reader's time. Know exactly why you're writing, then say what you need to say—like this example, where this writer respectfully requests an interview without preamble, fluff, or apology:

Hello, Sen. Smith,

I write an industry newsletter on the global supply chain distributed to thousands of professionals, and I know they're as curious as I am about your free-trade proposal.

See how easy that was? This writer shares their credentials and then gets right to the request—all in one sentence. Compare to:

Hello, Sen. Smith,

My name is Jeff Peters. I apologize for the cold email. I hope this message finds you and your team doing well. I'm reaching out because I work in supply chain logistics. I also write and publish a weekly newsletter that is rapidly growing in popularity. I believe my readers would appreciate your insights, and I would sincerely appreciate the opportunity to speak with you about . . .

Which message is more memorable? Which one is more likely to receive a response? Both emails are polite, but only one is concise.

Cutting down your greetings doesn't make you cold or impersonal. In fact, we insist you tailor your opener to the recipient:

Corra, your last newsletter made me laugh out loud, and it got me thinking about a partnership.

Another:

To Amanda and the team,

I've heard wonderful things about your catering services, and I'm hosting a dinner for 20 people on Saturday, Aug. 2.

And another:

Hi, Ian,

I've got a hundred questions after hearing you on *Fresh Air*, but I'll start with just one.

It's not impolite to be brief. In fact, it's considerate: You're respecting your reader's time.

Write an Irresistible Subject Line

The biggest factor in your decision to open an email is likely the sender, but in close second is no doubt the subject line. Of course, there are different categories of emails—personal, professional, newsletters, cold calls—but these tips will help you with all of them.

- **Don't duplicate the "from" line.** If the email is from Sam's Auto Repair, don't write a subject line that says, "A message from Sam's Auto Repair." Your subject line is too valuable to waste it with repetition. Say something that will get clicks, like "Half-price oil changes this week only."

- **Start with high-impact words and facts.** Don't bury the lede with "Oil changes for the next week will be half price." Write "Half-price oil changes this week only."

- **Create a sense of urgency.** People tend to decide right away whether to open an email. They rarely go back and consider them a second time. That's why, in the oil change example above, it's important to say "this week only." There's a deadline. Same with this example: "A burning question about today's podcast episode." But don't invent a sense of urgency if there isn't one. Subject lines like "Whatever you do, don't delete this" feel a *little* forward. (We're looking at you, political fundraisers.)

- **Keep it short.** If you write too much, your subject line could run off the end of the recipient's display, which is a little like talking on a voicemail until the recording runs out. "Get Post Malone tickets today" says enough to get people to click, assuming they like Post Malone.

- **Highlight one detail.** A newsletter from a museum offered this subject line: "New artifacts and online experiences." Zzzz . . . sorry, we dozed off there. More people would have opened that email if the subject line had read, "Diary of Betsy Ross's husband found in shoebox" or "Newfound diary details captivity of Betsy Ross's husband." Instead of trying to summarize everything, showcase a single interesting feature.

- **Beware of asking questions.** A journalism newsletter's subject line asked, "What's the deal with Sean Hannity's comments about vaccines?" At least we know what we're getting into if we click. But people read things to get answers, not questions, and wouldn't it be better for the subject line to give some clue about what we're going to learn? Maybe: "Hannity's pro-vaccine comments aren't appreciated at Fox News." OK, *now* we're curious.

- **Don't SCREAM.** Perhaps you're tempted to use all-caps because you want ATTENTION and you want it RIGHT NOW. But that's annoying, and it could trigger your email filter as spam.

- **Don't be afraid to name-drop in a business email.** If you're making a cold call via email in search of a job or some other business help and you were referred by a mutual friend, put that friend's name in the subject line: "Mindy Martin recommended your design services."

- **With bad news, be sensitive and direct.** Some people may think "Gus Jones died" is too blunt or cold, so they say something like "Sad news" and then force the recipient to open the email to see what's going on. Ever gotten an email like that? It feels terrible. You glimpse the subject line on the screen of your phone and panic, wondering what you're about to learn. It's better to say something gentle but straightforward, like "Rest in peace, Gus Jones" or "Honoring Gus Jones (1955–2024)."

- **Make your purpose clear.** A subject line saying "Just a reminder" won't remind your busy friend as effectively as "Reminder: Patty's party starts at 7 p.m. Friday." A subject line that says "A request" isn't nearly as grabbing as "Please edit my terrible draft."

- **Don't be mysterious.** A subject line for a political email announced, without context, "We're wearing the Daddy Badge." We don't know what that means, and we don't want to.

How to Address Someone in an Email

A surefire way to get your cold call email ignored is to open it with "To whom it may concern," "Happy Monday," or "Hey!" But avoiding a greeting altogether could be read as curt or impolite.

Here's how to formulate a greeting that's polished and professional.

- **Keep it brief and neutral.** "Hi there!" is perfectly appropriate for a brief check-in with a colleague. If you're writing for solicitation or business development, you should include the recipient's name: "Hi, Anna" or simply "Anna" will land better.

- **Use the right name and pronouns.** If the person has emailed you before, look at how they addressed you, as well as how they signed their message, and follow that. Otherwise, a brief Google or LinkedIn search can likely tell you whether your recipient goes by "Andrew" or "Andy" and whether they use he/him, she/her, or they/them pronouns.

- **When in doubt, defer to the more formal.** Formality is an indicator of respect, and earning respect is key to building relationships and credibility.

- **Triple-check that you got all names correct.** Misspelling names is a huge faux pas. Especially if their name is in their email address. Especially if you're emailing to ask them to do something. Like hire you. For editing.

Getting Noticed

Strong writing won't be read without strong headlines. And by "headlines," we don't mean just the ones in newspapers. Headlines also live online as banners, titles, social media posts, and subject lines.

If you're in the communication business and you struggle with headline writing, that's like having trouble breathing. You need to do it to survive. Consider this your oxygen mask.

How to Write Headlines That Grab Eyeballs

Here's a headline-writing exercise. Let's pretend we're editing an email newsletter for history nerds.

A writer has given us a cool story from 1902 that's 100 percent accurate (we swear) about how a guy in Oregon, Ellis Hughes, tried to steal a sixteen-ton meteorite, the largest ever found in the United States.

The meteorite sat three-quarters of a mile from his property, on land owned by the Oregon Iron & Steel Company. Hughes enlisted his fifteen-year-old son and a horse in an arduous effort to move the meteorite onto his land. They dug it out and slid it onto a flatbed cart that was rolled atop tree trunks serving as wheels. It took three months, but they did it.

Then they built a shack around it, announced the discovery, and started charging twenty-five cents apiece to take a look. One of the tourists was a lawyer for the steel company, and he was suspicious. He noticed the remnants of a path between the shack and a hole on the company's land. Oregon Iron & Steel sued and won, and the Willamette Meteorite now sits in the American Museum of Natural History in New York City. All Hughes got from his efforts was built-up muscles and legal bills.

Now let's write a headline and/or email subject line for the story. Here are some steps.

- **Start with keywords.** Identify a word or two that should be in the headline. For this one, it's easy. "Meteorite" is a must, and so is some word to convey the sneakiness—maybe "stolen" or "scam" or "plot."

- **Think about your audience.** If you're writing for lawyers, you might focus on the legal battle. If the audience is archaeologists or anthropologists, you might emphasize how ancient Native Americans worshipped at the meteorite. But your audience is fans of historical trivia who just want a good story. So give them one.

- **Write several headlines/subject lines for the story.** In the end, you may borrow pieces from a few of them to create your final product. At this early stage, you want several options that you can assess and improve:

The amazing story behind an enormous meteorite in Oregon

How a huge meteorite was given a wild ride on Earth

The arduous plot to steal America's biggest meteorite

**The meteorite scam: How a man, a boy,
and a horse failed to pull it off**

- **Tweak your first-draft headlines.** For example, make your passive constructions active, and rev up your language. Instead of:

  How a huge meteorite was given a wild ride on Earth

  . . . make it:

  How a huge meteorite took a mind-blowing ride on Earth

  Don't tease when the facts are compelling. Why say it's an "amazing" story? Instead, show it.

  People often skip emails when the subject line seems tricky. Instead of:

  The amazing story behind an enormous meteorite in Oregon

  . . . make it:

  The plot to steal an enormous meteorite in Oregon

  Be specific. "Enormous" is an opinion, not a fact. So make it:

  The plot to steal a 16-ton meteorite in Oregon

  Convey the story's tone. It's not a crime story. It's a story about human nature and how someone worked hard, only to fail. So make it:

The mad plot to steal a 16-ton meteorite in Oregon

Avoid unimportant details. It's not vital to know that the meteorite was in Oregon. So cut that:

The mad plot to steal a 16-ton meteorite

Don't use fancy words when more descriptive words are available. Instead of:

The arduous plot to steal America's biggest meteorite

. . . make it:

The backbreaking plot to steal America's biggest meteorite

Don't sacrifice clarity for cleverness, and don't try to be clever at all if the topic is grim. But in this case, it's OK to be a little cute. Instead of this one with the "pull it off" pun:

**The meteorite scam: How a man, a boy,
and a horse failed to pull it off**

. . . how about this:

**How a man, a boy, and a horse
shoplifted a 16-ton meteorite**

Note that "shoplifted" captures the reader's attention because it's unexpected: Who shoplifts something weighing sixteen tons? So it comes across as clever without sacrificing clarity.

Now eliminate the weaker headlines on your list. The finalists are:

The mad plot to steal a 16-ton meteorite

**How a man, a boy, and a horse
shoplifted a 16-ton meteorite**

**The backbreaking plot to steal
America's biggest meteorite**

Show the options to your colleagues. They may see something you don't. Good headline and subject-line writing is a team sport. Then pick one. If your social media post using the headline gets lukewarm interest, repost again with another angle and see if it does better. The internet can act as a litmus test (for better or worse).

Spill the Details

Now let's say you're writing a press release for a development company. Don't write something like this:

The St. Joe Company Releases a Video Showing Progress on Projects Currently in Development or Under Construction

No one thinks, "Oh, a video about generic projects. I can't wait to learn more about generic projects." Be specific. Use names and locations.

Let's look at more examples.

Kurt Gessler, former director of editorial operations for Tribune Publishing, lectures on headline writing. He's collected examples of headlines that underperformed online until they were rewritten into winners. Here's one example:

Local colleges offer students stress-busting activities

Here's the improvement:

Therapy horses, Bubble Wrap rooms aim to relieve college students' end-of-semester stress

Now that's a headline. We gotta know more about this therapy horse. And if you're worried about "giving away all the good stuff," you should worry about something else instead, like climate change or that weird rash on your leg. A quirky headline only gives people more reasons to read on. (And in this case, website traffic soared.)

An Indiana news website offered this headline:

**Attorney general files lawsuit
against Fort Wayne bridal store**

Hmm. Did the store fail to renew its business license? Did the owners forget to pay their taxes? The reader doesn't know whether it's juicy news or not. Try this headline, which makes it very relatable:

**State says Fort Wayne bridal shop
left 30 customers without dresses**

Get specific to help a story find its audience. That bad example at the start of page 103 could have said something like:

**Video: St. Joe Company Fuels Florida Panhandle's
Economy by Building Hotels, Stores, Marinas, 1,400+ Homes**

Tighten Up

You don't need to say everything in your headline or title. You just need to say one or two things well. Avoid secondary details that don't increase the story's appeal and may, in fact, obscure the details that matter.

A Chicago news outlet wrote this headline:

**Ald. Carrie Austin, chief of staff charged with
bribery in new federal indictment**

Some problems:

1. What's the chief of staff doing in that headline? The public doesn't care much about chiefs of staff.
2. What's "in new federal indictment" doing in that headline? Old indictments aren't news. If you want to make clear it's federal for some reason, "faces federal bribery charge" would work.

Why not find a richer angle? Here are some that were available:

**Carrie Austin, second-longest-serving alderman,
charged with bribery**

**27-year council veteran Carrie Austin
charged with bribery**

**Bribery charge makes Carrie Austin 3rd sitting
alderman under indictment**

State the most important fact, then go beyond that with a detail that places the news in the bigger picture. Make every word count.

Here's a headline out of Louisiana that needed help:

Louisiana officer with criminal history arrested again, charged with stalking

That's not terrible, but it is flabby. For one thing, you don't need to say "Louisiana" in the headline. Readers will assume it's Louisiana because it's a Louisiana news outlet.

Second, the headline doesn't give us any idea of what the officer's criminal history is. It's actually a number of things, but one of them is the same alleged crime as the new charge: stalking. So that's a good angle, and it's actually stated clearly in the fourth paragraph of the story. (When you write a headline for text that someone else wrote, don't be afraid to steal their best line. The most gripping angle should be used most prominently.)

So let's make the headline:

Officer faces 2nd stalking charge in 6 years

An improvement, right?

Just to get picky, let's note this Northern California headline:

Geoff Davis says nostalgia will be firmly on the menu at his new Oakland restaurant Burdell

What's the word "firmly" doing in that headline? Nothing. Nothing at all. So lose it, do a bit of rearranging, and you get:

Nostalgia will be on the menu at Geoff Davis's new Oakland restaurant Burdell

That's firmly better.

Use Subheads to Whisk Your Reader Along

Subheads are mini-headlines. They're the headers that pull you forward.

Recall the last time a friend told you an enticing, hilarious story. Maybe it was about her trip to Las Vegas. No doubt it was packed with telling details, juicy verbs, explicit adjectives—and subheads.

As your friend told her story, she delivered the first subhead after the drunken antics on the flight. She said, "Wait, it gets better."

The second subhead was "You won't believe the first thing we saw on the Strip."

The third subhead was "And that's when the bouncer arrived."

The fourth subhead was "By then it was midnight and 99 degrees, and there was the Bellagio Fountain."

And the final subhead: "I will neither confirm nor deny."

Your friend's "subheads" propelled you into each new chapter.

Subheads are just as effective on the page. Like so:

Forget the Reader, Save Yourself

A veteran writer we know starts any new project by writing potential subheads. He uses them as an outline. Subheads organize the scope and flow of a story, and can help you think.

Get a Bite, Reel Them In

Your main headline was relevant enough for the reader to pick up the report, open the email, or click on the link. Grabby subheads will get them over the too-long-didn't-read chasm and convince them to give your work the time it deserves. "Let me tell you about my trip to Vegas" got your attention. And then you stuck around to hear about the Bellagio fountain.

Rescue the Reader

Think of the last time you searched for a recipe online. You first spent forty-five minutes scrolling past the origin story of Uncle Barney's seven-alarm chili before you got to the actual instructions. Subheads rescue lost readers.

Highlight an Important Secondary Idea

You have a lot to communicate, and you can't cram it all into the subject line, headline, and opening paragraph. A subhead can alert the reader to a detail that might be otherwise buried.

One Final Note

Write your subheads with the same care as your main headline. If you find that you're struggling, take a hard look at that part of your article. Maybe you need to rethink the section. Or maybe your best course of action is to simply delete. In both cases, the subhead proved its worth.

How to Give a Presentation That Won't Make Audience Members Play Games on Their Phone

Research tells us that audiences remember the beginning of a presentation, the end, and not much from the middle. So make sure you nail the beginning. Here's how.

- **Give your presentation a descriptive title with powerful verbs.** Make your audience hungry to know more. If you're stuck, use the "how to" format, share one overarching idea, or go with a listicle:
  - How a book about mice transformed my work
  - How shutting up made me a stronger leader
  - Ten secrets to better small talk
  - Five reasons to take that big road trip

- **Make it interactive.** When audience members are using their brains, they're engaged. Find a way to include them as soon as you can. Make 'em raise their hands, participate in a poll, move around, interview each other, or play a game. (One of our favorite openers: Give everyone a pen and paper, and instruct them to tell a story about themselves using only visuals.)

- **Limit the text.** Don't make listeners read when they should be listening. Only display what is truly essential. Your presentation is merely a tool to aid your voice-over. The first slide sets that up.

- **Make it accessible.** Use soft background colors with text in a high-contrast color. Choose fonts that are easily deciphered. Start by searching online for "presentation compliance." It's the speaker's responsibility to make the presentation accessible.

- **Don't spend forever introducing yourself.** If you've got a long list of credentials—well, look at you, hotshot—ask someone else to introduce you. Your opening moments don't need to include your whole background; they only need to answer the question "Why am I in this room?" Hopefully the answer is something like "To demonstrate how data visualization can tell powerful stories," and not "I have no idea."

Chapter 3

Let's Format It

A 2008 study found that users typically read just about 20 percent on an average-length web page. (It's probably even less
now.) Imagine how much that percentage falls when you want them
to read something that looks like what's on the next page.

Compare it to the page after that—with indenting, bolding, subheads, and bullet points.

Both of these images feature the same words, but the second one
is much less intimidating. Much easier on the eyeballs.

The Hard-to-Read Example

Small Business Innovation

Another measure of innovation, particularly among small businesses, can be assessed through SBIR and STTR grants. Between 2010-2022, Illinois received 53 SBIR/STTR awards ($17M) for water technologies and Wisconsin received 27 ($9M) — comprising 3-4% of all SBIR/STTR awards. Some companies received more than one award (Table 14). By comparison, Massachusetts, which has a more established water sector, received 130 awards ($42M) — indicating that there is room for growth in innovation and commercialization within Illinois. In Illinois, 28 of awards went to companies with affiliations with University of Illinois at Urbana-Champaign. There were 13 awards that focused on water/wastewater treatment, and 11 awards that focused on contaminants in water.

While Illinois has incredible research strengths — its ability to commercialize research, among both universities and entrepreneurs—could be improved. Interviews with water industry stakeholders revealed challenges that the region can address, particularly for treatment and monitoring technologies, to improve commercialization and adoption of new products. These include: 1. Need for patient capital, given long commercialization times, to help collect data and prove out a concept, and implement new solutions at scale; 2. Access to pilot sites or some way to acquire test data for new technologies. Pilot sites can fill a gap between research conducted in universities and laboratories and commercial-scale development. Wastewater treatment facilities and industrial users are reluctant to buy new technology if there is no evidence of it working in a real-world scenario, and even better working for their specific application; 3. Technical assistance in establishing viable business and operational plans, particularly for scientists and engineers who have developed a new technology but do not have business experience to assess its marketability. Given the increased interest from investors and private-sector in water-related innovations (both traditional and tech-enabled), there may be momentum to increase innovation capacity and its adoption into the market.

The More Skimmable Example

Small Business Innovation

Another measure of innovation, particularly among small businesses, can be assessed through SBIR and STTR grants. Between 2010-2022, Illinois received 53 SBIR/STTR awards ($17M) for water technologies and Wisconsin received 27 ($9M) — comprising 3-4% of all SBIR/STTR awards. Some companies received more than one award (Table 14). By comparison, Massachusetts, which has a more established water sector, received 130 awards ($42M) — indicating that there is room for growth in innovation and commercialization within Illinois.

In Illinois, 28 of awards went to companies with affiliations with University of Illinois at Urbana-Champaign. There were 13 awards that focused on water/wastewater treatment, and 11 awards that focused on contaminants in water.

TABLE 14

Companies That Received More Than One SBIR/STTR Award

Company	Number of Awards
Serionix, Inc.	6
ANDalyze, Inc.	4
Eden Park Illumination, Inc.	4
Advanced Diamond TechNologies, Inc.	3
Dioxide Materials, Inc.	3
Cbana Laboratories	2
EP Purification, Inc.	2
Fluidic microControls, Inc.	2
NuMat Technologies, Inc.	2
QuesTek Innovations LLC	2

Barriers to Commercialization

While Illinois has incredible research strengths — its ability to commercialize research, among both universities and entrepreneurs — could be improved. Interviews with water industry stakeholders revealed challenges that the region can address, particularly for treatment and monitoring technologies, to improve commercialization and adoption of new products. These include:

- Need for **patient capital**, given long commercialization times, to help collect data and prove out a concept, and implement new solutions at scale.

- **Access to pilot sites** or some way to acquire test data for new technologies. Pilot sites can fill a gap between research conducted in universities and laboratories and commercial-scale development. Wastewater treatment facilities and industrial users are reluctant to buy new technology if there is no evidence of it working in a real-world scenario, and even better working for their specific application.

- **Technical assistance** in establishing viable business and operational plans, particularly for scientists and engineers who have developed a new technology but do not have business experience to assess its marketability.

Given the increased interest from investors and private-sector in water-related innovations (both traditional and tech-enabled), there may be momentum to increase innovation capacity and its adoption into the market.

How writing looks on the page is the difference between some-one reading or clicking away. So if you're working on a long report, memo, or presentation, ask:

What could you do to make it more visual?

Where could you add a photo, video, or chart?

Where could you add a quote or anecdote from a real person—instead of a generic or unsupported statement? (And maybe make the quote large and visible, like magazines do.)

Do all of this, and you'll invite readers in, not shoo them off.

Look at this box.
See? We got your attention. Formatting matters.

Organization for Emphasis

Hundreds of messages compete for our attention every day. We're always half-reading articles, emails, feeds, texts, and ads. Our attention is scattered—sorry, got a text; need to answer this. One sec. OK, back. Anyway, dedicated readers aren't that dedicated. They don't read. They scan, skip, and skim. That means you should make your writing *glanceable*—without sacrificing quality.

It's all in the organization.

Use the Return Key

You already have a fantastic shortcut at your fingertips: The return key.

Use it.

Let an idea sit on its own line.

It might be two sentences. It might be more.

Get used to your ideas hanging out there. By themselves.

Do not write long paragraphs that drag on and on and never end. Even if you have the best idea full of great meaning that will change the lives of every person who reads it. Even if you have motion and direction, without a single grammatical error. Even if you think all of those sentences are tied together. You aren't Shakespeare. And you aren't Chaucer, either. Even if you are the most verbose person you know, you must break up the paragraphs. See what we mean? With this really long paragraph? If you do not hit the return key, your readers' eyes will glaze over, and your words will get ignored.

Do your readers a favor and keep it short. Single-line thoughts help that.

Don't bury your ideas.

Call Attention with Bullet Points

To share important data, explanations, or instructions, you don't need long paragraphs.

You don't even need complete sentences. Use bullet points.

Here's a caption pulled from a university's Instagram:

> Saturday is our Alumni Arts Festival!
>
> This event connects current students, faculty, staff, and prospective students with alumni who work in the arts. The festival kicks off in Weiss Lobby with a networking event at 9 a.m. Lunch will follow on the quad at noon. Dance performances will be in Morris Auditorium at 3 p.m.

Not easy to absorb, especially if you're scrolling on your phone. Here's our rewrite:

> Saturday is our Alumni Arts Festival!
>
> This event connects current students, faculty, staff, and prospective students with alumni who work in the arts. Here's the schedule:
> - Networking event in Weiss Lobby, 9 a.m.
> - Lunch on the quad, noon
> - Dance performances in Morris Auditorium, 3 p.m.

Much more efficient, right?

Notice the bullet points follow the same format—event, place, time—which makes them the same length. Bullet points should be consistent. And short. (And, grammatically, no need for periods unless they're complete sentences.)

Bullet points are especially useful if you need someone to do something. No one likes doing things. So to get your audience to obey, flag instructions like this:

- Address is 950 W. Fulton.
- Reply to this email to RSVP.
- Please RSVP by Monday before noon.

Now, will your readers actually RSVP by Monday before noon? Probably not. But you've improved your chances.

Keep Left

Want to bewilder
your reader?
Want to turn your writing into a
maze because each line starts
somewhere new?

Then go ahead, center your text. But we don't recommend it. Centering lots of text makes your reader sprint back and forth like they're in gym class. You should only center headlines or one-liners. For instance:

Buy fifty more copies of this book.

The above is OK to center because we want it to stand out, and we want you to do what we say. And it's just one sentence.

If a statement goes past one line, make it a left-aligned paragraph.

Caption This

Photo captions are among the most-read words in print and online. Yes, believe it or not, people do read the captions. They might read nothing but the caption, in fact. So use the opportunity to make your point.

Here's how:

- **Write captions in present tense.** "The mayor marches in Sunday's big parade." You might make an occasional exception for historical photos.

- **Decide what content in the photo requires explanation.** Is it clear what's happening in the picture? Should you identify the people in the picture? Is the time or the place of the photo important? If something is not particularly important, it doesn't belong in your caption.

- **Don't state the obvious.** No need to write "Joe and Jill share a laugh." We can see that.

- **If the content of the photo is evident or if it's a generic photo from four years ago, use the caption as an opportunity to convey key facts.** Instead of "Mary Smith greets supporters at a political rally held four years ago," pick out an illuminating fact from the text and highlight it in the caption: "Mary Smith has raised a record-breaking $1.5 million for her reelection race."

- **Captions should be short and snappy.** No eight-word introductory clauses. Get in and get out.

    At the same time, don't keep your captions so short that they're uninformative. For example, rather than writing "Ron James hugs a coworker as he leaves his museum job," consider writing, "Ron James hugs a coworker as he leaves his job as the museum's first director of African art."

- **Don't forget to give proper credit to the photographer.** That credit line (usually in small type under the picture or in parentheses at the end of the caption) is the place to date the photo if necessary. For example: "(2017 file photo by Shondra Watkins)."

- **Make sure your caption and your main headline are working in tandem instead of repeating each other.** Some readers will read the headline, look at the photo, and then read the caption, so think of your caption as a sort of subhead.

- **When identifying people, you don't always have to be directional, like "third from left."** Sometimes that's the most efficient way, but it can also slow down the reader by forcing them to do math. Consider the simpler "standing" or "waving" or "wearing hat" if that's an option.

- **Don't just reread your caption before publishing.** Re-reread it. Then have someone else read it, just to be safe. It's a high-traffic item, which means any mistake will be extra excruciating.

How to Make Your Communication Look, Feel, and Sound Better

Never Go Out of Style

In writing, style encompasses two things: tone and mechanics.

Tone is your writing voice. It involves intention and precision, right down to word choices. David Sedaris is glib. Patent applications usually aren't.

The second element of style is mechanics—the technical parts. This involves rules for writing, like proper grammar and source documentation, which lead to the construction of a coherent paper, memo, or article.

Here's a real-life text message among business associates about social media content:

> tbh i'd keep it up bc it's like the only day to post it bc it's
> halloween content (obvi lol) but maybe ask her?

A bit hard to parse, yes. But this text message is a great example of modern writing. Grammatically it's breaking rules, but it's got something important: style. (It might not be *your* style, but it's still got style.)

So what makes it stylized? What makes it sound that way? Those broken grammar rules! No capital letters. No periods because periods are considered stern in texts. Plenty of abbreviations to speed the point. Plus a friendly "lol" to soften the request. This style isn't right for a grad paper, obvi. But it still works.

So what style is right for your writing?

Three prominent stylebooks exist to guide you: *The Chicago Manual of Style*, the *MLA Handbook*, and *The Associated Press Stylebook*. The goal of each of these stylebooks is not to stifle creativity or potency of language, but to set standards to maintain the quality of writing and research. Organizations like university departments or businesses typically pick one of the main books to follow.

AP Style vs. Chicago Style: Some key differences

	AP	CHICAGO
Oxford comma	Don't use it The dog eats, sleeps and plays	Use it The dog eats, sleeps, and plays
Em dashes	Use a space before and after She was a good dog — but not all the time.	No spaces She was a good dog—but not all the time.
Ellipses	No spaces between periods She was a good dog ... until the squirrel incident.	Add space between periods She was a good dog . . . until the squirrel incident.
Titles	Use quotes "The Call of the Wild"	Use italics *The Call of the Wild*
Accents	Don't use them No dogs allowed in the cafe.	Use them No dogs allowed in the café.
Numbers	Spell out through 9 There were nine dogs at the park.	Spell out through 100 There were one hundred dogs at the park.
Some proper noun possessives	Don't use "s" with singular proper nouns ending in "s" Have you seen my dog Charles' chew toy?	Use "s" with singular proper nouns ending in "s" Have you seen my dog Charles's chew toy?
Over vs. more than	Don't use over More than half of all dogs are considered overweight.	You can use either Over half of all dogs are considered overweight.
Academic degrees	Use periods Charles is so smart, he should have a B.A., M.D. and Ph.D.	No periods Charles is so smart, he should have a BA, MD, and PhD.

And we have good news: Stylebooks aren't designed to be read cover to cover. They're reference books. *The Chicago Manual* and *MLA Handbook* tell you how to footnote, how to incorporate quotations into prose, how to punctuate, and, importantly, how not to plagiarize. They focus heavily on academic writing but are used by businesses, too.

The *AP Stylebook* also covers punctuation and writing tips, but the primary audience is journalists, not academics, so the focus is different. A big chunk of the book is an A-to-Z guide to capitalizations and abbreviations.

Journalistic style emphasizes clarity and ease of reading. Eliminate jargon and clichés, AP exhorts. For example, AP is trying to eliminate the vague term "officer-involved shooting," which is police jargon that reporters have adopted. Better to say exactly how the police officer was involved in the shooting.

If you appreciate clear writing—which you obviously do, because you're reading this right now—how can you not love AP style? And yet, there is controversy.

Please take a deep breath and contemplate your place in the vast universe before reading on.

Let's Have a Big Fight About the Oxford Comma

The Oxford comma is the comma that goes before "and" or "or" in a list. For example, "blueberries, strawberries, and boysenberries." Some people think the last comma is unnecessary.

MLA style and Chicago style advocate for it. AP style says to skip it. These two sentences show why it matters:

I'm traveling to Saugatuck with my two best friends, Bruce Springsteen and Justin Bieber.

I'm traveling to Saugatuck with my two best friends, Bruce Springsteen, and Justin Bieber.

The first sentence makes it seem as if Springsteen and Bieber might be your two best friends. The second sentence—with a mere comma added—makes it clear that the famed singers are not your best friends and that your best friends are tagging along. (What a treat for them.)

People who oppose the Oxford comma say almost all sentences are clear without it. After all, everyone knows Springsteen and Bieber are not your best friends. And even the anti-Oxford AP says you can add the extra comma if it means avoiding confusion.

Nonetheless, the Oxford comma debate has raged for decades, provoking tears and tantrums in writers everywhere.

We're using the Oxford comma in this book, which has upset a few of our writers who really ought to get a grip.

How to Make a Slide Deck That Isn't Ugly

Strong slide decks communicate your ideas, hold the audience's attention, and more importantly, translate into results. Bad slide decks make you look like an idiot.

Here's how to not look like an idiot.

First, ask yourself these questions and write the answers down:

- What is your audience excited to learn? (If you don't know, find out.)
- In just one sentence, what's your headlining banner idea?
- What one fact or concept do you want the audience to walk away knowing?
- How are you going to get them there?

Talk these questions through with your colleagues. Make sure your topic is compelling. Design can make captivating content soar, and it can even give dry content a lift. But it can't rescue you from a topic that's completely bland.

Now, on to the design. The strongest slide decks are simple and beautiful. To get there:

- **Use only a few words per slide.** Pick a punchy thought, display it in big type, and have the speaker (you) deliver the juicy details or supporting information. (Bonus: This also makes you a better presenter. You're forced to really know your stuff.)

- **Break it up.** If you really need more words to get your point across, parcel them over multiple slides. No paragraphs. No sentences, even. Too many words on the screen and your audience will half-read the screen and half-listen to you, and soon you'll lose them completely. Don't divide their attention.

- **Select the right fonts.** If you're lecturing on, say, health disparities among racial groups in the United States, choose a professional font to match the seriousness of the topic. If you're debating *Star Wars* versus *Star Trek*, you're free to use a font with some personality. But no matter what, pick fonts that are clean, legible, and can be read from the back of an auditorium.

- **Carry the visual theme throughout.** Select a palette of three colors and stick to it. No surprise pink flowery clip art on a slide if you're talking about women (for many reasons).

- **Use strong, emotive photography.** Google will lead you to troves of free or inexpensive stock images—but don't just grab the first cheesy image you see. If your photo features someone wearing a suit, beaming, and giving the double thumbs-up, go in another direction. And when you do add photos to your presentation, ensure they're not warped or pixelated, which is caused by stretching them. Adobe is our go-to source for stock images: stock.adobe .com. The first ten are free. (Adobe did not pay us to say this.)

- **Don't fear charts and graphs.** Try representing information in an unexpected way. If your plan was to drop in a bar chart from somewhere on the internet, understand the data and re-create it yourself.

- **Use smooth transitions between slides.** We love a dramatic screen wipe as much as you do, but best to stick to the conservative options.

- **Cut the excess.** Clean is better than distracting. Do you *really* need that drop shadow there? What about that fireworks animation— are you sure? You do? OK. Just checking.

Here are two examples of badly designed slides and the improvements we made to them.

Badly designed slide:

Good Presentation Content delivery

> To make a good and successful delivery of your content, include concise, clear messaging that focuses on the core values of your organization. To do this, you must remove the jargon, use repetitive language, and add pauses for emphasis. Try not to repeat your statements verbatim, instead clean it up and make it clear for the reader. It's about what gets heard, not said.
> - Jargon may be well known to you in your organization, but your audience will not understand. Acronyms and big words, too, add to confusion and delay in comprehension.
> - By repeating the same phrases, you help to drive home the important messages you intend your audience to retain.
> - Pausing for emphasis lets people know that what you are about to say (or have just said) is important and they should focus on the information.

Improvement:

Badly designed slide:

Which snack category is growing the fastest?

	2018	2019	2020	2021	2022
Salty snacks	136,987	192,421	865,309	3,999,993	9,529,144
Chewy treats	800,000	2,000,000	4,000,000	5,500,000	6,000,000
Organic bites	525,600	989,811	2,000,000	7,654,321	7,800,800

Improvement:

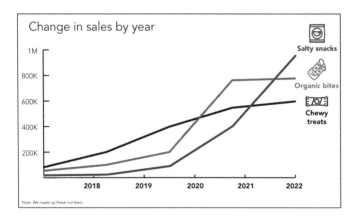

Great presentations are much easier to show than explain. We've curated a few for you to download on our website at mharris.com/GreatPresentations.

Choose the Right Typeface

The words "typeface" and "font" are frequently used interchangeably, but they have different definitions. Knowing this will impress the designer in your life, so here you go: A typeface features an alphabet, numbers, and punctuation that share the same design. Papyrus, for example, is a typeface.

A font, on the other hand, is a set of glyphs *within* a typeface.

That means 8-point Papyrus is a font. And 184-point Papyrus is a separate font. But they're the same typeface, and why are you using 184-point Papyrus, by the way? This we gotta see.

Let's go deeper. Here's a quick primer on the three most basic typeface forms:

Serif: The name says it all. These typefaces use serifs. For the uninitiated, the dictionary explains that a serif is "a slight projection finishing off a stroke of a letter in certain typefaces."

A design teacher once told us to imagine serifs as feet and arms. Little people right there in the typefaces.

You're probably familiar with the serif font family of Times New Roman. Glance at it here and see what emotions it evokes. Feels classic, doesn't it?

Serif typefaces typically set that tone—sophisticated and durable. Elegant and authoritative. Serifs are a nod to the history of ink-on-paper.

Sans serif: This means, of course, without a serif.

Sans serif typefaces can often feel more modern; they're less fussy without all those feet and arms. Helvetica is a well-known sans serif. Ever shop at Crate & Barrel? Flown American Airlines? Then you have seen Helvetica in some form.

A common trend is to use sans serif fonts to denote the new and modern. Sans serifs are all over the internet.

Yet they can also feel reliable and sturdy. Like good building blocks.

Script: These are typefaces designed to look like handwriting.

Scripts appear handmade. Less mechanical, more human. The Coca-Cola wordmark is a famous use of script. It's short and memorable with that bold, happy red.

Why know all this? Because having a typeface vocabulary can help you convey the mood you want for a project. For a formal project, for example, a serif typeface is most appropriate.

For a project that's more conversational, try experimenting with a script or a bold sans serif. And if you want to frighten people, use Webdings.

Size Up

Many guides for email typography will encourage you to set your type at a minimum of 12 point in an email. Provided the user is standing still, we agree. But your intended audience could be reading their phone while walking, jogging, or doing jumping jacks. With this in mind, the guidelines set forth by the overlords at Apple and Google dictate a minimum size of 14 point for paragraphs.

This means that reasonably sized title or headline typography should begin at 18 point and scale upward conservatively as needed.

These sizes might seem constrained, but you are ensuring the focus remains on your content and not on the design decisions you've made.

Finally, remember that your users are likely using accessibility features on their devices if they prefer larger or smaller typography. The guidelines here will enable your content to take advantage of those user settings, increasing the likelihood of your message being received.

Be Bold—Sometimes

Bold-faced type should draw attention to a key point of information or call to action.

For example, you're writing an email to a senior manager. The intent is to share three updates on your project.

Here's a good use of bold:

Good morning, Sheila,

Here are a few updates on our accounting project:

1. Completed the review of all accounts payable
2. Submitted a new policy on company reimbursements
3. Analyzed the largest past-due accounts

I'm concerned about my findings in the largest past-due account. **Can I get a half hour on your calendar this afternoon to meet and discuss?**

The action step is highlighted. We all get too many emails, and readers are trained to find only the most important information. Use bold to prioritize their reading.

Link Up

The intent of using hyperlinks is to guide the reader to go deeper in a particular subject matter. Links work best when they feature multiple keywords.

Here's what we mean.

Good, helpful, easy to read: Here are <u>the dos and don'ts of baking gluten-free cookies</u>.

Poor, difficult, easy to miss: <u>Here</u> are the dos and don'ts of baking gluten-free cookies.

Search Engine Optimization (SEO)

If your goal is to rank high on Google's organic algorithm, we recommend including a multi-word link like the one above in the first, second, and third paragraph of your content. Our SEO expert, Nathan Misirian of Autumn Consulting, found Google's algorithms typically "read" up to three paragraphs of text while simultaneously scanning for links.

Don't Yell

Audiences don't like to be SCREAMED AT.

That means no all-caps messages. No screaming—even if you believe your audience *deserves* to be screamed at.

See there? We just proved italics are better, if used sparingly. But in general, let the flow of your sentence create your emphasis. (Pro tip: Put your strongest point at the end of your sentence for that extra snap.)

As for capitalization in general, follow established rules:

Proper nouns are capitalized.

Common nouns are not.

You should capitalize when they appear before a name, like this: *Executive Editor Sarah McDougle.*

And then lowercase titles that come after a name.

So if an editor uncapitalizes your title, please know they're just following the rules. They are not trying to make a statement about your importance.

If you capitalize randomly, you will evoke an ex-president who once tweeted, "I capitalize certain words only for emphasis, not b/c they should be capitalized!"

Which explains this twenty-car pileup:

@realDonaldTrump

Despite the Democrat inspired laws on Sanctuary Cities and the Border being so bad and one sided, I have instructed the Secretary of Homeland Security not to let these large Caravans of people into our Country. It is a disgrace. We are the only Country in the World so naive! WALL.

When you capitalize random words, you're making the reader's inner voice rise and fall at all the wrong moments. SO DON'T DO IT!

Add an Email Sign-Off

Every email you send for work should end with an email signature. That's the bit at the bottom that contains your basic information. It might look like this:

P. T. Mane

Unicorn Wrangler

Horns R' Us

555-555-5555

ptmane@hornsrus.org

Think of it as your digital business card. It will help people search through their emails and find you later. What's P.T.'s phone number? I know it's here somewhere . . .

Go to "settings" in your email program, add a signature, and it'll be automatically appended to every email you write from now on. (You'll also need to do this on your phone settings.)

Here are some dos and don'ts:

- **Do** include basic information like your name, phone number, email, title, and company. Just the facts; no need to publish a novel.

- **Do** choose a font that is large enough to read on a phone; at least 12 point but preferably 14. (See earlier entry on font sizes.)

- **Don't** make the mistake of choosing a distracting or unreadable color. Black is safe; grays and many blues are hard to read; red will scare people.

- **Do** consider adding a small company logo.

- **Don't** sweat it, though. If it's too hard to upload the logo or it doesn't look good on mobile, drop it. It's not necessary.

- **Do** consider adding links to your primary social media platform if social is really important to you.

- **Don't** use religious or political quotes as signature lines in your work emails. It's best to steer clear of those topics—unless you're actually a religious or political figure.

- **Do** remember that a signature line is a very valuable little piece of real estate. It's a small billboard that goes out to dozens, maybe hundreds, of people a day. And if you have something to market or sell, that is an opportunity. Just think of how many times you've read "sent by my iPhone" at the bottom of an email.

So if your new book just came out, or if your client's sexy new bar is opening next month, write some snappy ad copy and add it to your email signature line.

And voilà, a free ad automatically goes out to everyone you're emailing.

Chapter 4

Let's Fix It

We already talked about formatting, and how order and space encourage readers to stick around. But even the cleanest formatting can't fix the real problem, which is this:

Your emails are too long. Your briefs are not brief. And your invitations are uninviting.

You're writing too much, and no one reads long writing. No one. Basecamp CEO Jason Fried put it best: "Short paragraphs get read, long paragraphs get skimmed, **really long paragraphs get skipped**."

Concise writing attracts and holds readers. Here's some guidance and practice exercises in getting people to actually read and absorb your meaning.

Advice on What to Do—and Not Do—for Effective Communication

Don't Say the Same Thing Twice or Be Redundant

Pop quiz! Spot the redundancies in this sentence:

> He and his wife, Patricia, started a GoFundMe to help raise money, but then they received an unexpected surprise.

GoFundMe is a well-known fundraising tool—so no need to have "to help raise money." And then there's "unexpected surprise." If it's a surprise, it's already unexpected. It's like a "free gift." If you've got a friend who gives you a gift and then charges you for it, that's not a gift, and that's a crappy friend. (You could also cut the word "help" before "raise.")

Now try to spot the redundancy here:

> Due to their importance, there is wide scientific interest in understanding how glaciers evolve over time.

Of course evolving occurs over time. That's the definition of "evolve." They're the exact same thing. Aha! *Exact same* is redundant, too.

Here, have another:

> Fort Detrick Police have neutralized an active shooter situation involving an armed gunman.

Not only is the "active shooter" described unnecessarily as an "armed gunman," but the phrase "armed gunman" is redundant, too. Unless you know some gunmen who aren't armed.

Now let's put you to the test. Identify the redundancies in this paragraph:

> The proliferation of zebra mussels (*Dreissena polymorpha*) in Lake Michigan poses a grave ecological and economic threat. These invasive mollusks, native to the Caspian and Black Seas, have established a formidable presence in the Great Lakes region, including Lake Michigan, through rapid colonization and fast population growth. Zebra mussels' capacity to adhere to various surfaces, such as water intake pipes, boats, and native mussel shells, results in clogging and impairing the functionality of vital infrastructure and industrial facilities.

We were able to cut forty-one words. Here's our rewrite:

> Zebra mussels (*Dreissena polymorpha*) in Lake Michigan pose an ecological and economic threat due to colonization and population growth. Zebra mussels can stick to surfaces like water intake pipes, boats, and native mussel shells, impairing vital infrastructures.

Here's another. This is a recap of an environmental conference. It's got sixty-seven words.

Cut as many as you can without sacrificing the meaning:

> We undertook several rounds of in-depth, not-for-attribution interviews with corporate executives, financial community

leaders, and key stakeholders to identify perspectives on sig-nificant issues and challenges facing the clean energy transi-tion. The interviews sought to garner views across the range of current and potential investor types to develop an under-standing of areas of consensus and divergence about why such financial actors participate—or choose not to—in solu-tion investments.

And our rewrite:

We interviewed financial leaders about why they would or would not invest in the clean energy transition.

As you can see, we are brutal.

Don't Overuse Acronyms

Let's start with the overuse of acronyms, also known as OOA.

Writers can save words and get to the point by employing widely understood acronyms, or WUAs. But when they use acronyms that aren't crystal clear (ATACCs) or when they fill a sentence with multiple acronyms (MAs), they create an unappetizing alphabet soup, aka UAS.

Here are some headline examples:

**PPP vs. TARP: Which program offers
the biggest ROI for taxpayers?**

Did they have to use that third acronym? Couldn't they have said "Which program is better for taxpayers?"

**HGC, DCConnect Global, and QLC Chain
complete successful trial of MEF LSO APIs.**

MEF is a digital industry group. LSO is Lifecycle Service Orchestration. API is Application Programming Interface. (Are you still reading? Did your eyes glaze over?)

Granted, in a technical publication like the one where this headline appeared, many readers know these acronyms. But does everyone? And even if it can be deciphered, the headline looks like a word jumble.

**TRI-AD and DMP Kick Off HD
Map Update PoC from April 2020.**

This is a headline for a press release directed at people interested in technology, so maybe the writer can be forgiven for assuming that PoC always means proof of concept. But it can also mean point of care, people of color, point of contact, and prisoner of conscience.

We've given you three examples of headlines, but acronymitis is also a major problem in regular text. While occasional use of common acronyms makes sense, it can quickly spiral beyond comprehension.

Acronyms are jargon that lets some readers in but shuts out the rest. Fight back. Don't write a sentence that looks like a dump truck full of letters spilled its load, aka a DTFLSL.

A note: Before you send us an angry email, know that we're using the word "acronym" in the loose sense. Some language purists say an acronym is composed of the first letter or letters of a phrase in a way that makes a pronounceable word, such as NASA or FOMO. These purists say a collection of first letters that cannot be pronounced like a word and instead is pronounced one letter at a time—such as FBI or ATM—is an initialism. Our point: No matter what you call them, overuse is bad.

Hold It

There's a reason the most famous example of a bad opening sentence is, "It was a dark and stormy night."

"It" is a soft and vague way to start a sentence. After all, who or what is "It," apart from an evil clown?

We're not saying to never start a sentence with "It." If the meaning of "it" is clear from a previous sentence, it may be just fine. We're just asking you to make it rare.

Yes, we know some great writers started novels with the word "It." ("It is a truth universally acknowledged, that a single man in possession of a good fortune, must be in want of a wife," wrote Jane Austen in *Pride and Prejudice*.) But it's a truth universally acknowledged that none of us are Jane Austen.

Recognize Hyphens vs. Dashes

A hyphen is used to connect words. A dash separates them.

Use a hyphen to link two adjectives that come right before a noun. For example, you ate pancakes at the all-night diner, or you pulled an all-night study session. "I stayed up all night" doesn't need a hyphen, because there's no noun to describe.

As for dashes: Consider them an interruption—like this. You use them to bring attention to an amazing detail without muddling your message.

Unfortunately, some writers throw words between dashes because they can't figure out how to organize the sentence.

Here's a particularly awful example:

> Only winless Vanderbilt and LSU—which self-imposed a bowl ban in hopes of drawing sympathy from the NCAA after its investigation into sexual abuse is settled—are missing out.

There are twenty-two words inside the dashes and only eight words outside of them. The phrase between dashes swallowed the sentence. Gulp.

Also, it's unclear whether both Vanderbilt and LSU were winless and whether both schools self-imposed a bowl ban. In fact, only Vandy was winless and only LSU imposed a bowl ban. Here's an easy rewrite that solves both problems:

> Two teams are missing out: Vanderbilt, which went winless, and LSU, which is facing a sexual abuse investigation and banned itself from the bowls to gain sympathy from the NCAA.

Dashes are powerful tools for emphasis and clarity—wield them well. And not too often. If you use many of them in a row—like this—they lose their verve.

Here's a rule: Any sentence with four commas or more is a good candidate for a rewrite. See whether moving a clause or breaking it into a second sentence can get rid of some of the commas and dashes, thus improving the flow.

Banish "Apparently"

Apparently, we have a problem: Writers are misusing "apparently" all the time.

According to *Merriam-Webster*, it means "something that appears to be true based on what is known." But in practice, it's used to throw doubt on a report that a news outlet thinks is somewhat shaky.

Some headlines:

Apparently, Ivanka Trump is learning to play guitar during her free time

This is based on a single fact: Ivanka said she was learning to play the guitar. So why not just report that Ivanka says she's learning guitar? That way, you're not taking her word for it or doubting her word—you're just saying she said she is learning guitar. Which is true. (Do you think she knows "Smoke on the Water"?)

Kim Kardashian is officially richer than Kylie Jenner, apparently

If it's official, you don't need to say "apparently." In this case, it's based on a *Forbes* list, which is very unofficial. Why not just say it's from a *Forbes* list, or that a list of the wealthy puts Kim ahead of Kylie?

Bill Belichick is wearing two masks, apparently at all times

Wait a second. Unless you're with the Patriots coach at all times, how can you say this, or even say it's apparently true?

Apparently Freddie Mercury's mother
wanted him to be something else than a musician

The problem with this headline is that the late Queen frontman's mum is quoted directly in the story as saying: "I wanted Freddie to be a lawyer or an accountant or something like that."

So what's the word "apparently" doing there? It's unnecessary, unless you think Freddie's mother is a liar.

Go Easy on the Ize

Scientists, bureaucrats, instruction manual hacks, and even journalists are terrified the word "use" belittles their oh-so-distinguished writing. So they supers-ize it into the much more officious "utilize."

Take the *New York Times*, for example:

> They have also started a nonprofit, Paradise Stronger, which **utilizes** their background in fitness coaching to bring mental health care to residents coping with trauma from the disaster.

A *Science* magazine headline:

> **Gut microbiota utilize immunoglobulin A
> for mucosal colonization**

State of New York website:

> Stavatti Aerospace, Trek, Life Technologies and Sucro Real Estate NY to **utilize** low-cost power for economic development projects in Niagara and Erie counties

"Use" is completely acceptable. It means the same thing, and it's a shorter word with fewer syllables. Your job as a writer is to convey meaning, not show off.

Don't Turn Nouns into Verbs

Scaffolding, dialoguing, friending—some writers are simply hell-bent on turning nouns into verbs. It's a phenomenon known as "verbing." (Just kidding. Please don't call it that.)

Here's a new one that we find particularly horrifying: laddering. From an Indeed job posting:

> Convenes resources, builds alignment and implements a variety of communications programs laddering to the employer brand content . . .

And a blog headline:

Laddering: A Technique to Find Out What People Value

What people value is clear language. Better to use "linking," "connecting to," or "syncing with." Meanwhile, garage the laddering. Unless you need to reach a kitten who is treeing.

Don't Go to the Well Too Often

Successful writing can be simple and conversational. But overly chatty language tends to trivialize what you're writing. In the cases below, the writers interrupted themselves to drop in the word "well":

> It was killed because it was acting oddly and because, well, giant rat equals heebie-jeebies.

> I prefer the breadless bowl version because, well, carbs.

> With MAD no longer soliciting non-Sampson material, its idle creatives got, well, creative.

This use of "well" is sort of a drumroll that makes the reader expect something clever after it, but many writers leave only disappointment.

Same thing with "um":

> As with everything involving Kuznetsov, it's, um, complicated.

> The New Moon in Virgo occurs on September 17, and it's, um, a lot!

In both cases, using "um" feels like a desperate attempt to sound laid-back and casual.

Here's a bonus tip: Don't include the "um"s when you quote someone. That's, um, a waste of a word.

Fix Your Bad Writing, Don't Just Acknowledge It

There's one thing worse than using tired, old expressions, and that's telling readers that you know your expressions are tired and old and then using them anyway. Three examples:

> It has become an overused term, but he's the GOAT.

When you think a term is overused, why use it? Are you counting on everyone else to stop using it so you can keep using it?

> It's a cliché, but it really is true that children are our future.

No one said clichés weren't true. They just said clichés were tiresome.

> I know people always say time of possession is incredibly important, but in this game, it really was.

If people always say it, don't. Apologizing for bad writing before you commit bad writing does not absolve you of the crime.

Don't Self-Insert

Football coaches who find end-zone celebrations annoying sometimes say, "Act like you've been there before." The same goes for writing something clever. Don't act surprised or impressed by your turns of phrase. Don't call attention to them. If they're truly clever, people will get them. If they're not, best to just keep moving.

If only an editor would've saved an entertainment writer from this opening sentence:

> March is certainly coming in like a lion with a king's share of events (see what I did there? Somehow I feel the need to apologize to Nathan Lane and Nathan Lane only. Anyhow). While some of our venues are slowly opening up, there are still some online shows that deserve your attention.

Is the story about *The Lion King*? No. Is the story about this writer's meta experience while writing a routine events roundup that she didn't care about? No. It's supposed to be about events. So why not start off with an event or two?

This is an example of self-absorbed writing. Ego as enemy. Subordinate the self. Make the content the star.

Don't Overwork Your Metaphor

Try to follow the metaphor in this lede from a major news outlet:

> After years of slowly easing toward remote work arrangements, companies and their employees had to take the plunge fully clothed in March. Instead of drowning, they learned to make it work, saving an untold number of jobs and ushering in profound changes that will carry into a post-pandemic world.

Wowza.

The writer was discussing remote work, but because of the overwrought metaphor, readers were probably thinking about naked or clothed people jumping into water, and whether they drowned or not. His metaphor carjacked his lede.

And because you're a trained editor by now, you must have noticed that his paragraph has too many words. Why put "slowly" in front of "easing"? Is anyone ever "rapidly easing"? And "an untold number of jobs" means the same thing as "jobs."

Here's a simpler, less problematic lede:

> The trend toward remote work grew slowly for years—until last March, when it suddenly became the only answer for many. The impact for employers and employees will endure long after the pandemic subsides.

The takeaway: Be clever when it helps you make your point. But be careful that it doesn't distract from it.

Don't Make Sweeping Statements

Be careful when you issue declarations that include words and phrases like "always," "no one," or "never."

A sports columnist wrote:

> Now there is talk about expanding the College Football Playoff from four teams to twelve. No one is saying it, but it is all about generating more TV revenue.

Really? *No one* is saying it?

The Associated Press wrote six days earlier, "The television rights for a proposed 12-team playoff could be worth about $1.9 billion annually."

USA Today also wrote six days earlier, "Possible CFP expansion could increase revenue to more than $2 billion."

Many clearly knew and said that TV revenue was a key motivator. It's not that no one was saying it—it's that the columnist wasn't listening, was too lazy to check, or wanted to act like he was ahead of the game when he wasn't.

This is just one example of why making sweeping statements can be perilous, especially when you're declaring that something has never happened.

Here's another example from a major East Coast newspaper:

> No one ever said that learning to ski or snowboard was particularly fun or easy.

But a US national ski group says: "It's fun and easy to learn how to ski."

And an Italian ski school says: "Learning to ski is fun and easy."

And a New Hampshire ski website says: "Our new Bebe Wood Free Learn to Ski & Ride Program makes it fun and easy."

We'll admit: Proving that newspaper wrong was fun and easy.

Bow to the Royal Order of Adjectives

What makes Queen's "Crazy Little Thing Called Love" such a great song? Besides the '50s rockabilly sound, catchy chorus, handclaps, scorching guitar solo, memorable melody, and other good stuff, that is.

Queen knew the Royal Order of Adjectives.

Imagine if this 1980 No. 1 hit were called "Little Crazy Thing Called Love." That doesn't have quite the same ring to it, now does it?

The Royal Order of Adjectives, or adjective order for us peasants, dictates the specific order adjectives must appear in a sentence, based on their category.

On the next page are those categories, in correct order.

The Royal Order of Adjectives

ORDER		EXAMPLE	WRITE YOUR ADJECTIVE
1	Determiner	Technically not an adjective, a determiner appears before the adjective and is considered a part of the Royal Order. Example: a, the, our, these.	_____
2	Quantity	one, three, 654	_____
3	Opinion	tasty, comfortable, beautiful	_____
4	Size	tiny, thick, gargantuan	_____
5	Age	young, ancient	_____
6	Shape	round, spherical	_____
7	Color	red, purple	_____
8	Origin	Austrian, German	_____
9	Material	steel, cotton	_____
10	Qualifier	The last, often most important adjective, sometimes called purpose. Think, *bicycle* race, *theme* park.	_____

Going back to Queen's "Crazy Little Thing Called Love": "Crazy" falls into the opinion category, so it appears before size, "little." If Queen were for some reason singing about their teenage love lives, it would be "Crazy Little Young British Thing Called Love." Sounds like a hit to us.

You now might be asking yourself: Shouldn't Queen use commas between all those adjectives? Yes and no.

If the string of adjectives comes from different categories like in Queen's song, don't use a comma. If two or more adjectives come from the same category, separate them with a comma.

Queen was a gifted, successful band. ("Gifted" and "successful" are both "opinion" adjectives.)

Know When to Use a Comma

If the phrase starts with "which," use a comma. This holds true 99 percent of the time. Maybe more. In fact, in the rare case where "which" might not be the best choice, it is still defensible.

Consider these examples, which are both correct.

The software, which we are offering at a discount to new clients, will ensure your network is secure.

The software that is based on our proprietary technology will ensure your network is secure.

We suspect most writers go by ear when they choose "that" or "which," and do so correctly, but here's an easy way to think about it: If the information you're adding is important in defining and understanding the word or phrase it follows, you're going to reach for "that," and you won't need a comma.

In the second example, the fact that your company developed the technology is crucial. It singles out this software from its competitors. You don't want anything to come between the reader and that fact, not even a comma.

That's it. Feel free to dig deeper, researching restrictive and nonrestrictive clauses, and you'll find exceptions, but you can also just remember to use a comma with "which" and feel proud of yourself every time.

Know Who vs. That

How you use "who" and "that" in your writing can set you apart, identifying you as a discerning writer or tagging you as a sloppy one.

If you're referring to people, use "who." It's as simple as that. Well, nothing in English is all that simple, but this one is pretty clear.

> My first boss, who had a fiery temper on deadline, was otherwise pleasant and friendly.

> The CEO has always said the people who work in the warehouse are the backbone of the company.

Some esteemed grammarians, including Benjamin Dreyer, whose *Dreyer's English* is an absolute gem, argue this rule isn't ironclad. He cites the Ira Gershwin song "The Man That Got Away" in showing that groups and unnamed people can be "that"s. That may be, though taking word usage cues from songs sounds dicey. The bigger issue is deciding how you want to sound.

Consider the following example. It's a memo to employees trying to show empathy. It gives off a chilly mood.

> We want to celebrate family and loved ones that have supported our employees through this difficult period.

Especially when compared with this:

> We want to celebrate family and loved ones who have supported our employees through this difficult period.

Distinguish yourself. Be the writer who uses "who" and "that" correctly.

Be Considerate

Show sensitivity in your writing: Don't use mental health terms as descriptors. Refusing to wear a seat belt isn't "deranged." But it is foolish and dangerous.

That three-point shot at the end of the game wasn't "insane." It was superhuman. Crushing. Dramatic.

The weather is not "bipolar." It's unpredictable.

Words like "crazy" or "demented" are easy to reach for, but reach an inch further—it's worth it.

Stay Ahead of the Law

What you write can easily be forwarded, misdirected, screenshot on X, sent to HR, or subpoenaed.

So what should you keep out of emails? The list can be both exhaustive and exhausting. Hopefully we do not need to remind you not to send compromising photos or your bank account number.

Here are four less obvious but no less dangerous areas to avoid:

1. **Jokes:** Save 'em for your Netflix special. What you send could be confusing (some people don't get sarcasm even when it's spoken) or worse, offensive.

2. **Threats or ultimatums:** Don't email while under the influence of anger (or under the influence of anything, for that matter). Write your tirade, then wait ten minutes or an hour or a day before sending—or not sending. Let your cooler head prevail.

3. **Nasty comments about a colleague:** Keep those thoughts to yourself or share them with your pet iguana. Nastygrams sometimes end up being shared with the colleague in question or forwarded to HR.

4. **Off-the-cuff advice:** No one knows that the business advice you just sent was typed as you watched your kid's soccer game while calling in a pizza order. They'll think it's the real deal. Wait until you can concentrate.

Before you hit send, always reread what you wrote and follow this valuable advice: Never put anything in an email that you wouldn't want to see in giant type on a screen in a courtroom. You want your emails to be memorable, not actionable.

Spare Us the "Helper" Verb

In school we learned about "helper verbs," auxiliary verbs that work with other verbs. Those "helpers," however, often hinder our meaning.
Consider:

> "They were able to complete the course . . ."
> *vs.*
> "They completed the course . . ."

The first conveys only the ability, not the fulfillment of the task. The second, by stating the action, implicitly conveys the ability to do so. The same idea holds true in these examples:

> "The governor took the opportunity to congratulate . . ."
> *vs.*
> "The governor congratulated . . ."

> "The vice president decided to promote . . ."
> *vs.*
> "The vice president promoted . . ."

> "Within weeks, company officials began instituting new protocols . . ."
> *vs.*
> "Within weeks, company officials instituted new protocols . . ."

Say what you mean—clearly and unambiguously.
One further thought: Let tenses do the work.

He will retire later this year.

She was promoted earlier this month.

In those cases, "earlier" and "later" offer no additional information, just vagueness.

Harness the Power of Analogies

Analogies paint vivid imagery and understanding. At their strongest, analogies distill complicated topics for nonexperts.

Try parsing this:

> This powerful software is the vital security solution that all
> your networks need for robust vulnerability assessment.

Bored yet? How about confused? Also, is that supposed to be marketing lingo? Because we're not feeling motivated to go buy the product. We're not even sure what the product *is*.

Let's rewrite with an analogy to compare the software to something much more well-known—something any audience will instantly understand.

> This software is your castle's walls, moat, and knights.

> It holds the firepower of a battleship.

> As secure as an armored car.

See? Analogies are a powerful weapon to add to your arsenal.

Trim Long Openers

Here are two lead paragraphs in articles by a veteran writer for a metro news outlet:

> For more than a century, every generation has had its cinematic adaptation of "Black Beauty," and while the new Disney+ version switches the genders of the magnificent horse as well as the young protagonist and moves the locale from the English countryside of the late 19th century to the American West of today, it's thematically and spiritually faithful to Anna Sewell's timeless classic, from the horse serving as narrator to the episodic nature of the storyline to the powerful and still-relevant message about humane treatment of animals—and the undeniably healing and lasting dynamic between human and creature.

Was he paid by the word? Because that paragraph has ninety-nine of them.

Another opener by the same writer:

> John Belushi's life story has been told again and again, and yet the documentary "Belushi" (premiering Sunday on Showtime) is an original and particularly captivating chronicle of the star-crossed comic genius' life and times, thanks in large part to a treasure trove of audio interviews with friends and colleagues and loved ones of the Wheaton-raised legend, including Dan Aykroyd, Jane Curtin, Chevy Chase and Lorne Michaels, as

well as the departed Harold Ramis, Carrie Fisher and Penny Marshall.

That's an eighty-word sentence. Miles too long.

We don't want to be too hard on this writer. Both of these sentences are constructed sensibly so you know what the writer is saying. Perhaps he's just trying to become known for a quirky personal writing style. Or maybe it's a search-engine-optimization play to cram search terms into the tops of his stories.

But sentences—especially lead sentences—should make readers feel welcome, not like they're signing a contract to take out a thirty-year mortgage.

It's true that William Faulkner once wrote a 1,288-word sentence, and he won a Nobel Prize. But unless you're William Faulkner, keep your sentences much tighter than this. Short sentences are easier to understand. And pack a punch. Right? Right.

There's No There, There

In the movie *Ocean's Eleven*—the 2001 remake, that is—Brad Pitt's character tells a rookie,

> "Don't use seven words when four will do."

Solid advice. Here's a shortcut to follow it.

Look at the start of your sentences. Do you see the word "there"? Cut it! You're only delaying the crux of the sentence.

"There will be congressional hearings this year" changes to "Congressional hearings are scheduled for fall."

"There are new documentaries coming out on Netflix this weekend" changes to "New documentaries are coming to Netflix this weekend."

"There are times when I'm in the mood for a heist movie" changes to "Sometimes I want to stare at George Clooney's chiseled jawline."

Think Again

Next time you find yourself writing "I think," don't.

Ironically, the phrase "I think" suggests you might also *not* think. It undercuts the authority of whatever follows.

> I think the decision to play winter sports at this time is wrong.

> I think it's time for electric jets to replace today's jets, just as electric motors have destroyed traditional internal combustion engine vehicles.

If you're writing or saying a thing, rest assured your audience will perceive your words as conveying what you think. Same goes for the word "believe."

And a note to writers quoting other people: You often can drop "I think" in quotes, too—for the same reason.

An exception: "I think" can be useful if you're contrasting your beliefs with those of others or intentionally expressing uncertainty.

Otherwise, lose it.

Get the Facts in Order

How you order facts in a sentence makes all the difference between success and failure.

For example, a DC journalist's tweet:

@journalist

The CDC director will announce guidelines for what vaccinated people can do during the White House coronavirus briefing at 11 a.m.

This sentence seems to say that the CDC chief will advise people on how to behave while the briefing is going on. A simple rewording fixes it:

@betterjournalist

During the White House coronavirus briefing at 11 a.m., the CDC director will announce guidelines on safe activities for vaccinated people.

In this lead, the writer found he had a few facts left over and tacked them to the end:

@journalist

Then-President Donald Trump urged the chief investigator of the Georgia Secretary of State's office to look for fraud during an audit of mail-in ballots in a suburban Atlanta county, on a phone call he made to her in late December.

The lead includes a clumsy comma trying to patch over its construction problem, but still, it seems to say that the audit took place on a phone call. A simple rewording:

@betterjournalist

Then-President Donald Trump called the chief investigator of the Georgia Secretary of State's office in late December and urged her to look for fraud during an audit of mail-in ballots in a suburban Atlanta county.

Writing a sentence packed with facts is not easy. So much is competing for emphasis. After you write something like this, read it over slowly and make sure nothing can be misconstrued.

After all, if you say you're writing an article on elephants, you don't want people to think you wrote it while sitting on elephants. Unless you did.

Banish Blob Words

Most of the sentences people write will invariably and often contain a huge number of unnecessary words.

Or to put it another way:

> Most ~~of the~~ sentences ~~people write will invariably and often~~ contain ~~a huge number of~~ unnecessary words.

William Blundell, author of *The Art and Craft of Feature Writing*, dubbed useless words "blob words." He wrote: "Some words and phrases are blobs. Others are paint brushes whose narrow meanings instantly create pictures in the reader's mind. They are specific and concrete, not general and abstract."

A sharp writer is a blob-word hunter. Let's attack this sentence:

> All employees should really believe that asking questions is simply the best way to succeed.

If you mean "all employees," just say "employees." It's clear you're referring to all of them. And what good is "really" doing in the phrase "should really believe"? Either they should believe or they shouldn't—there's no middle ground. Next is the often notorious word "that." Sometimes "that" is necessary, but it's often a blob word. Read the phrase or sentence without "that" and see if it makes sense. If it does, your "that" is a blob.

The first eight words of the sentence can be reduced to five: "Employees should believe asking questions . . ."

Now tackle the rest of the sentence: ". . . is simply the best way to succeed." The word "simply" raises a red flag. Ask yourself: Is what I'm describing the best way to succeed or not? It's one or the other. The word "simply" is litter. So lose it.

Now meet your new, de-blobbed sentence: "Employees should believe asking questions is the best way to succeed." You just axed four useless words.

Don't Just Cut Words—Cut Syllables

Too many people think the only way to make your writing concise is to use fewer words. But there's more to it than that. Think syllables, not just words. It's actually a two-step process.

Let's go through an exercise with the following paragraph:

> The woman took a break from her job as a police officer directing traffic and decided to make a stop at the gymnasium to exercise. She had just arrived at that location when she received notification that a fire was burning inside her single-family residence. She traveled home in a hurry, arriving there just in time to witness the fire spread to the garage that served as the storage space for a 1948 Chevy Fleetline that she had long treasured.

Now let's cut down the number of words from eighty-one to forty-three without losing any important facts:

> The traffic cop was about to start her lunch-break workout at the gymnasium when she received notification that her house was on fire. Rushing home, she arrived just as the blaze reached the garage where her treasured 1948 Chevy Fleetline was located.

Much cleaner right? But let's lower our syllable count to speed it up even more:

> The traffic cop was about to start her lunch-break workout at the gym when she got word that her house was on fire. She

made it home just as the blaze reached the garage where her prized 1948 Chevy Fleetline was parked.

The word count is the same, but we just took out ten syllables—the same number as in the word "anti-materialistically"—with no loss of information.

We're not saying that monosyllabic words are always best. You don't always have to replace "attempted" with "tried." But quicker is generally better. It's the gift of time to the readers.

Don't Misplace Your Modifiers

Bet you didn't know there's a subgenre of bad grammar jokes about misplaced modifiers walking into bars. For your enjoyment:

> "A misplaced modifier walks into a bar owned by a man with a glass eye named Ralph."

> "A dangling modifier walks into a bar. After finishing a drink, the bartender asks it to leave."

Sidesplitting.

These awful jokes do point to a common and embarrassing mistake, though: Writers often lose track of their nouns and then attach descriptions to the wrong ones. Here's an especially nonsensical variant, in which a sports team's flags are driving cars:

> While driving around, some Razorback flags were spotted flying and a few cars had Hog decals.

The writer thought he was referring to himself but wasn't. Always make sure introductory clauses like that are followed by the noun you actually mean to modify.

Kindly "But" Out

An easy way to link two thoughts is to throw the word "but" between them. Problem is, "but" suggests that the second thought is in opposition to the first, and if it isn't, the sentence is a mess. An example from a local news outlet:

> We are moving into uncharted territory with partisan school board races in Nashville, but it's well established that teachers matter more than any other element in student success.

The writer wanted to get across the idea that partisan school elections might hurt teacher recruitment. But the writer didn't say that. A decent rewrite:

> Some people in Nashville see benefits in partisan school board races, but it might hamper recruitment of teachers, who matter more than any other element in student success.

Here's another example of bogus "but" use:

> While it may seem ill-advised to experience the hottest place on Earth during the hottest season of the year, Abby Wines, a Death Valley spokesperson and park ranger, said that March, April, July, and August are Death Valley's busiest times, with roughly 100,000 visitors each month. But those who choose to visit this time of year do so for several different reasons, she said.

What's "but" doing at the start of that second sentence? Get out of here. Shoo.

Declutter

Cluttered writing reflects cluttered thinking. If you can't simplify a topic, you probably don't understand it in the first place.

Here's the first paragraph of "sponsored content" by a major US corporation:

> In 2020, digital tools have been a lifeline for small businesses. As the pandemic struck, igniting the era of social distancing and

pushing Americans' lives—and shopping habits—even further online, small business owners who have relied on technology to place and fill orders, communicate with customers, accept payment and enable contactless pickup or delivery have stayed ahead of the game. They have become digital entrepreneurs.

Not only does the second sentence have fifty words, it has a lengthy clause with a phrase between dashes crowding the middle. It needs a road map. And some periods. There's no ration on periods. Use 'em, don't lose 'em.

Here's a rewrite that cuts the sixty-six-word paragraph down to forty-four and simplifies the message:

Our partners have been working together for decades. Our purpose is providing the highest quality work product with the care and attention you would expect from an owner of the company.

The pandemic pushed Americans' shopping habits further online. But social distancing didn't require small businesses to ignore their customers. Smart businesses used digital technology to place and fill orders, communicate with customers, accept payment and enable contactless pickup or delivery. They became digital entrepreneurs.

The most informative part of that paragraph was the list of ways in which digital technology can boost business. Putting that list at the end of a serpentine sentence buried it. The rewrite, on the other hand, highlights it.

Another example, taken from an "About Us" on a company website.

Our partners have been working together for decades. Our purpose is providing the highest quality work product with the care and attention you would expect from an owner of the company.

Though over time our tools and methodology have continued to improve, our principles have remained constant: to provide policyholders with all the expertise they need from a company they can trust. As an independent firm that specializes in loss accounting, we provide the guidance and the skills to get the job done right, the first time.

We need a nap after laboring through that paragraph.

So what's special about this business? We have no idea. And neither does the writer. Let's cut the jargon and try this again:

We'll guide you through every step of claim preparation. With more than three decades of experience in loss accounting, we follow one principle: Never miss a detail.

There we go. A focused, clear snapshot and nothing more.

Do the Right Thing

"Thing" is one of those English words we can't live without. We use it without much thought. But you want your writing to actually say something, and "thing" doesn't usually say anything.

Some examples from news sources:

Staying motivated to keep things clean around the house can be difficult, especially with a jam-packed schedule.

Remove the flab:

Staying motivated to keep the house clean can be difficult.

Another example:

Once workers are required to be in the office each week, it could put downward price pressure on things like boats, campers, and second homes—which all sold briskly during the move to remote work.

Cut "things" or be precise, replacing it with "big-ticket purchases." Here's another:

There's a confluence of things happening in different locations around the world that are all contributing to problems in many different industries, from computer chips to fuel supplies to furniture.

Whoa. Admittedly, "things" is just one problem with this example, but it gets the sentence rolling, at least. Here's an improvement:

Worker and product shortages globally are contributing to supply-chain issues in many industries, including computer chips, fuel, and furniture.

Be Mindful About Non-English Words

Foreign words or phrases, even those commonly used in English, can add color and sophistication to your writing—or confuse the hell out of readers.

Case in point from an online sports story:

> The fans give college football its verve, its *je ne sais quoi*.
> (Somewhere here there is some combination of *Notre Dame*
> and *je ne sais quoi* that would be most appropriate. Is it *le je ne
> sais quoi de Notre Dame?*)

Come again?

This version of Notre Dame is in Indiana and the use of *je ne sais quoi* is silly. The phrase literally means "I don't know what" in French and is borrowed by English speakers to mean an indefinable quality. The writer should have stopped at "verve."

Even sillier is the pitch for a pheromone-infused cologne for teenagers that the writer tells us is:

> A warm but refreshing scent that's sure to give your teen that
> certain *je ne sais quoi*.

Whoa. Pheromone-infused cologne for teenagers seems like a very bad idea. But it's the *je ne sais quoi* that's the real head-scratcher.

You get the point. When you are trying to be witty, use words that you actually understand, and not words tossed in to seem erudite. You want to avoid a *faux pas*.

Use Parallel Structure

Even as infants, humans detect patterns in their environment. Patterns promote learning: sunrise to sunset, lullabies and bedtime, the 1,372nd reading of *Goodnight Moon*, letters, numbers, geometry, grammar.

Writers should use patterns like parallel structure to ensure their work is understandable.

Parallel structure means using the pattern of words to help the reader more easily organize and process the information. Used correctly, parallel structure introduces clarity and places emphasis where you want it. Faulty parallel structure is like a broken bulb in a string of lights: The whole presentation falls apart.

Here is an example of parallelism gone awry in a comparison:

> Which is why the message about diversity in a historical perspective is just as important as how that message is presented.

The phrase "is just as important as" demands similar sentence elements for a proper comparison. Here we have a noun "message" compared to an adverb "how." An easy fix:

> Which is why the message about diversity in a historical perspective is just as important as the presentation of that message.

Correcting this mistake can punch up a list. Here's an example of a set of instructions that meanders because one bullet starts with a verb and the other with a preposition:

You can turn on character counting on your iPhone so you know how many characters each text message is before you send it.

- Tap the Settings icon, and scroll to the Messages option.
- In the Messages section, tap the button to the right of Character Count to turn it on.

Bulleted lists should begin with the same part of speech: noun, adjective, verb, etc. Above, one bullet starts with a verb and the other with a preposition.

Corrected:

- Tap the Settings icon.
- Scroll to the Messages option.
- Scroll to Character Count.
- Turn on Character Count.
- Never mess up parallel structure again.

Don't Mistake Identities

Beware of attributing actions to the wrong people. Three examples:

> The referees and Trae Young got an earful from Nets head coach Steve Nash after the former drew a series of cheap fouls last night.

Who is "the former"? Did the referees draw fouls?

> A Whitfield County Sheriff's Deputy escorted a Channel 3 crew out of a public town hall meeting Wednesday night and threatened them with arrest after attempting to ask Rep. Marjorie Taylor Greene a question.

Why did the deputy try to ask Greene a question?

> Twitter suspends Trump permanently after inciting mob (cable news chyron)

Why did Twitter incite the mob? Shouldn't Twitter suspend itself? Whenever you write a clause that contains a verb, make sure the verb is connected to the right noun. The examples above are easy to fix:

> Nets head coach Steve Nash gave an earful to both the referees and Trae Young after his player drew a series of cheap fouls last night.

A Whitfield County Sheriff's Deputy escorted Channel 3 journalists out of a public town hall meeting Wednesday night and
threatened them with arrest after they attempted to ask Rep.
Marjorie Taylor Greene a question.

Twitter suspends Trump permanently for inciting mob.

Cut Wimpy Words

"Really" can have great impact when spoken. Written? It's a speed bump on the way to making a point. "Really" and its friend "very" are imprecise and almost always unnecessary.

In each of the following newspaper headlines, "really" minimizes the impact:

**Do we really understand
the Second Amendment anymore?**

**It's no surprise we're refighting the Civil War—
it never really ended**

Not to be outdone, "very" also waters down the writing. To prove this point, a friend of ours advised substituting "damn" for "very" to see just how silly it sounded:

**What determines a perfect cup of coffee is
very/damn subjective**

Here's another weakening word: "clearly."

When someone writes a headline like "Dodgers: Max Scherzer clearly 'furious' after Clayton Kershaw single," you have to wonder why the person is using the word "clearly" if it's clear. It seems argumentative, as if the writer thinks it's clear but fears the reader won't agree. Lose it.

Throw Away the Stale Metaphors

Consider this sentence on a financial research website:

> Should you hop on to the Beyond Meat (BYND) bandwagon or
> hold your horses just yet?

That crusty old metaphor about holding your horses is especially inappropriate because, if you're ordering food without meat, you're already asking the cook to "hold the horses."

But the writer probably didn't even think about that. The writer just wanted to get across the idea of waiting and used what linguists call a "dead metaphor" or a "frozen metaphor." That's a figure of speech that's so familiar it no longer does what a metaphor is supposed to do: Create an image in the reader's mind.

Use metaphors that feel fresh, modern, and relevant. If you want to describe how overwhelmed with work you are, don't say you're "burning the candle at both ends." Say you feel like you're triple-booked with Zoom meetings and you can't get yourself off mute.

We can't all be great writers. But at least we can be original writers. Take some chances. Invent your own metaphors.

Clichés
and Other Common Blunders

Let's start with clichés. Here's how to use them:

Don't.

Never use 'em. Ever. Clichés are the junk food of writing—they've got no nutritional value. They're a failure of imagination, and you can do better if you just think outside the box.

Aha. That was a cliché. Didya catch it? "Think outside the box" doesn't inspire, motivate, persuade, or evoke any emotion whatsoever, does it? You skimmed that and felt nothing. Except perhaps boredom.

The goal of writing is to convey meaning that sticks in the reader's memory. Anything that detracts from your meaning or makes it forgettable must be cut.

Here's how to spot clichés and then replace them with richer, more purposeful writing.

The Future Is Now

Here's one we see everywhere: "The future is now."

If it's supposed to be an attention-getter, it's failing. It's distracting. And meaningless. It's a scourge in tech and science writing in particular. Take a look at these examples, pulled from headlines:

**The future is now: Long-term research shows
ocean acidification ramping up on the Reef**

**The Future Is Now: Firefighting Robot
Battles LA Fire for the First Time**

**Skills are the currency of the future,
and the future is now**

We tried to hunt down the origin of this phrase, and the earliest usage we could find was the name of a documentary from 1955. It should've stayed there.

At the End of the Day

The overused phrase "at the end of the day" has a literal meaning that sounds appropriate only for evening use.

"At the end of the day, we are only human."

Then what are we in the morning?

"At the end of the day, it's all worth it to her."

And if she feels differently at lunchtime?

"At the end of the day, we are neighbors."

Before 5 p.m., we are not neighbors?

Plus, every character counts, so why use twenty-one characters when "ultimately" accomplishes the same thing in ten? "Eventually" works, too.

"At the end of the day" is litter. Let's tidy up.

Now More Than Ever

"Now more than ever" is meant to sound lofty and important, but it is neither. From the headlines:

Why Going Outside Matters Now More Than Ever

Now More Than Ever, Words Reveal the Past

Kids Need Superheroes Now More Than Ever

This became the most overused phrase of 2020. (Besides "you're on mute.") We get why. It's an attempt to acknowledge that things were unusually awful (and they were).

But instead of "Now more than ever, we need media literacy training," just say—directly and succinctly—why that is:

We need media literacy because of rampant misinformation spreading online.

Done.

A Perfect Storm

**Scientists fight to avoid a perfect storm
of fungal infections**

**Expert explains why Washington weather
makes perfect storm for mosquitos to thrive**

**The Yankees are walking into the perfect storm
with more position news for next week**

Some headline writers think any combination of anything is a "perfect storm." It isn't, so instead, name the actual causes and the effects. Like this:

**Spread of fungal infections and increased
drug resistance raise alarms**

**Warm weather and melting snowpack make
Washington welcome for mosquitoes**

Big bats coming back to power Yankees into playoffs

If you do use "perfect storm"—sparingly—please remember that it should describe a dangerous thing, not something that will boost your batting average.

Out of an Abundance of Caution

Next, out of an abundance of revulsion, we nominate "out of an abundance of caution" for the most needless phrase of the English language. This phrase floods news accounts and announcements without teaching anything new.

CNN:

> Sen. Patrick Leahy (D-VT) was hospitalized out of an abundance of caution, just hours after presiding over the opening of former President Donald Trump's second impeachment trial.

A Texas school district:

> While we await the results for the individual, out of an abundance of caution, the student and parent are under self-monitoring and social distancing at home . . . The parent and student did not return to campus after visiting the Houston Rodeo.

A hockey team press release:

> **Blackhawks Cancel Practice**
> **Out of an Abundance of Caution**

Nice to know that athletes who regularly punch each other in the head are being careful.

"Out of an abundance of caution" increases your word count without actually saying anything. Cut the cliché and give us the "why."

**Blackhawks Cancel Practice
to Minimize Risk of COVID-19 Exposure**

Remains to Be Seen

It's admirable when writers point out gaps in their knowledge. But it's less admirable when they say they don't know facts that no one could possibly expect them to know, employing that well-worn phrase "it remains to be seen."

For example, a website for lawyers writes about a newly filed lawsuit:

> It remains to be seen whether any of these allegations have any merit.

Duh. That's why we hold court in the first place.

Meanwhile, a major newspaper assesses an NFL draft prospect:

> But it remains to be seen if his talent will translate to the NFL.

You mean we don't know how a guy who hasn't even been drafted yet will do in the NFL? Shocking. Next you'll tell us it remains to be seen which team will win next year's Super Bowl.

A Tale of Two

Charles Dickens had a vivid imagination. But when he published *A Tale of Two Cities* in 1859, could he possibly have imagined that writers still would be recycling his title all these years later? Like this:

A tale of two restaurants

**A tale of two trios that will open the Saturday lineup
of the Springfield Jazz & Roots Festival**

A tale of two halves for Bears offense

In as few words as possible, what is it you want your audience to know? *That's* what you write.

**One restaurant closes,
another next door opens its doors**

**Saturday at the Springfield Jazz & Roots Festival:
fusion and old-time New Orleans jazz**

The Bears suffer after a powerful opening half

Ho Ho Horrible

Perhaps people's creativity runs out around year's end? Because these clichés are a holiday tradition.

'Tis the season to go jogging

**'Tis the season: How Patriots players
gave back this holiday season**

'Tis the season for ransomware

And there's the belief that any positive occurrence before the holiday is an "early Christmas present."

Hurricane Sally widow gets early Christmas present

**Kids get early Christmas present
when dad returns early from deployment**

Election was early Christmas present for Republicans

Don't threaten to add anyone to your naughty list, don't warn people that they better watch out, no reminders that 'tis the night before whatever—these are as dry as holiday ham.

Further considerations:

- It's not "seasons greetings," it's "season's greetings"; the greetings belong to the season, showing possession, so there's an apostrophe.

- Don't wish someone a merry Christmas; wish them a Merry Christmas, with a capital *M*.
- We wish our friends Happy New Year; not a Happy New Year's.
- And there are many ways to spell the Jewish holiday, but the two standard spellings are "Hanukkah" and "Chanukah."

Secret Sauce

The Jack in the Box fast-food restaurant chain popularized the term "secret sauce" in the 1970s, seeking to inject a note of intrigue in its war against the Big Mac. Since then, secret sauce has been slathered on so many ideas that we gag when we read it. Here's the dreaded phrase in a news story:

> For Peloton, the leaderboard technology it aims to protect
> is the secret sauce of connected fitness.

Here's an example in a headline:

What's in a Newsletter?
At the *Times*, There's a Secret Sauce

Call it what it is: Secret. Confidential. Exclusive combination. Alchemy.

Leave the sauce in the bottle.

Beating a Dead Horse

It feels like beating a dead horse here, but BC has struggled to run the ball all year.

Not only is this phrase icky, but the writer is admitting that he's saying something everyone already knows. He's going to put himself out of a job!

A longtime Mountain View resident has founded a new non-profit she hopes will kill two birds with one stone: feeding local families in need while supporting struggling restaurants.

Are they going to eat the two birds, then?

Nikola Jokić's superpower is that he does it his way, which is slow, methodical, and precise. There's more than one way to skin a cat.

You won an NBA championship. Go ahead and celebrate. But why torture a cat, too?

Try these three sentences instead:

Fans have grumbled all year about BC's struggles to run the ball.

A longtime Mountain View resident has founded a nonprofit she hopes will have two major impacts: feeding local families in need while supporting struggling restaurants.

Nikola Jokić's superpower is that he does it his way, which is slow, methodical, and precise. There are lots of paths to the finish line.

Clichés hide meaning. And when the topic is really important, they're insensitive, too.

In Other Words

Does the phrase "in other words" add meaning or flavor? See this paragraph about a successful internet personality:

> She's one of the first women to co-own an esports organization, and she's earned over 3.5 million subscribers on YouTube, her streaming platform of choice. In other words, her career is going well, and she's worked hard to get there.

Anytime you write "in other words," you're admitting that you are repeating yourself. It also delivers a subtle insult: It assumes the reader was too dense to understand the concept the first time around. (And if you ever *do* decide to insult your reader, make it really good.)

Another example, from an article about cooking:

> This delectable dish is crunchy, buttery, and addictive. In other words, it's delicious.

No one needs to read the same thought twice. And no one needs to read this same thought twice, either.

Like a Broken Record

New car prices breaking records has become
a broken record for car shoppers in the past year.

At risk of sounding like a broken record, I am once again
required to inform you that the housing market is heating up.

I've felt like a broken record nearly every time
I've written about Motorola.

Why do reporters insist on using this phrase? Maybe it's a cry for help. Maybe they're trying to signal to us that they, too, are sick of the same boring stories.

Unfortunately, if the writer is bored, so is the reader. "Like a broken record" is dead space in a sentence. It's antiquated, and it's only getting more antiquated with new technology. Soon enough, no one is going to know what it means.

So let's leave it in the past. Where it belongs.

Years Young

**Hosman is 94 years young, and no one is more
excited about the inductions than him**

**At 100 years young, Anna Ciolini's advice is to "eat right,
exercise and try to do the best you can"**

Director Mel Brooks Is Now 95 Years Young

**At 102 years young, Sidney Walton, a World War II veteran,
is raising money for frontline nurses**

This phrase hasn't been fresh and clever for at least one hundred years.

Look, you can put "95 years young" on Aunt Liz's birthday cake. That's nice of you. But writing is different. It's supposed to reflect deeper and more sophisticated thinking.

After all, you need to think outside the box and avoid low-hanging fruit even when you're rushed. If you're unsure whether your writing is too cliché ridden, run it up the flagpole so that, when push comes to shove, you don't get thrown under the bus.

Conclusion

S it back. Take a few deep breaths. Then climb outside your body. Remove yourself from your writing so you can see your words as others will.

In fact, stop thinking of them as *your* words. You're not judging yourself. You're just judging words. You're doing what's necessary to serve your audience.

And that's what matters most—the audience. How will they feel? Perplexed? Surprised? Compelled to read on?

Will the writing have the desired effect? And what is that desired effect anyway? If you don't know, it's impossible to determine if the writing succeeded or failed.

Once you finish the first draft, immediately stop thinking of yourself as the writer. Put distance between yourself and the text. Become the editor.

Everybody needs one of those.

Contributors

Project management by Willa Reynolds
Illustrations by Sean Anthony Mack
Charts by Jonathon Berlin
Finance: Mitch Hirt
Agent: Monika Verma, Levine Greenberg Rostan Literary Agency
(We love you!)
Editor: Ronnie Alvarado, Simon Element

Writers

Jenn Bane

Stephan Benzkofer

Rachel Bronson

Chris Courtney

Lynn Davy

Tania deLuzuriaga

Marie Dillon

Tyeesha Dixon

Ralph Frammolino

Eunice Han

Writers (continued)

Jane Hirt

Rex Huppke

Mark Jacob

Cristi Kempf

Jara Kern

Scott Kleinberg

Michael Lev

Matt Mansfield

Charles Meyerson

Nathan Misirian

Brian Moore

Kevin Pang

Rob Reinalda

Gretchen Reynolds

Mary Schmich

Liz Shields

Sharon van Zwieten

Acknowledgments

O n my first day of high school journalism class, my teacher turned off the lights, leapt on a student's desk, and flung a textbook out the window. You don't learn journalism out of a textbook, he bellowed. You can only learn it by doing it.

That teacher was Dean Hume at Lakota East High School in Liberty Township, Ohio. I need to thank him and the many teachers and editors who did more than improve my writing—they lifted my career.

For more than forty years, Roger Boye has run the high school Cherubs program at the Medill School at Northwestern University. That program and four more years at Medill taught me that relentless editing is the best editing. My assignments came back **bloodied**.

Chuck Clark, then an editor at the *Indianapolis Star*, lobbied to put me on a front-page story when I was a twenty-year-old intern. That got me noticed by Timothy Franklin, who hired me for an internship and then my first job out of college at the *Orlando Sentinel*. He hired me again at the *Baltimore Sun*. Now senior associate dean at Medill, Tim remains a sounding board more than two decades later.

Sal Recchi in Orlando, Andrew Green in Baltimore, and Michael Lev at the *Chicago Tribune* were kind bosses and tremendous line editors. They coached as they critiqued.

Jane Hirt, to whom we dedicated this book: When I met Jane in 2009, she was the managing editor of the *Chicago Tribune* and approved my hire. Nearly a decade later, I reconnected with her during her "radical sabbatical," in which she took a year off from work and said "yes" to most everything, from ramen-making classes to improv comedy training. Seeing an opening, I made a big ask for her to fill in for me while I was on maternity leave and never stopped asking. I'm so grateful she keeps saying yes.

And Eric, Olivia and Ellicott, and Mom and Dad: I love you.

—Melissa Harris

I'm indebted to the stubborn and uncooperative people in my life who don't believe me when I say I don't know what I'm doing.

I'm forever grateful for Siena, Lucca, and their voices, and for Christine, Trin, Jane, and Melissa for helping me find mine. My gratitude and love go to Nadija, Lynne, Scott, and our Chicago family for decades of support and laughter.

Jon, thank you for a lifetime of adventure, and the adventure of a lifetime.

—Jenn Bane

To our editors:

We recommend the team at Simon Element to any aspiring writer. Starting at the top, they are publisher Richard Rhorer; editor in chief and fellow Cherub alumna Doris Cooper; our go-to editor, Ronnie

Alvarado, and assistant editors Emma Taussig and Maria Espinosa. Our partnership has been pain-free, and how many editors can you say that about?

Mark Jacob read our work before the team at Simon Element did, which no doubt eased the pain. Our colleague Mary Schmich wrote this about Mark upon his retirement from the news business:

> If I had to sum Mark up in adjectives, I'd say: curious, patient, impassioned, a touch manic, tenacious, sincere, trustworthy, and hardworking . . .
>
> And loyal.
>
> "Mark's got your back" is a phrase often heard in the newsroom. He gave loyalty and earned it in return.

Mary won the Pulitzer Prize for Commentary in 2012 with Mark as her editor. We have no delusions that this book will reach the same heights, but having him in our corner has been reassuring to us, too.

We would add one more adjective to Mary's list: "wise." When Mark suggested changes in this manuscript, he always provided meaningful and considerate reasoning. And when writers don't get words right, trouble follows. So thank you, Mark, for helping us avoid embarrassment. For now, anyway.

—Melissa and Jenn

Index

About the Authors

Melissa Harris is the founder and CEO of M. Harris & Co., a Chicago-based marketing agency. She spent fifteen years as a journalist at the *Orlando Sentinel*, the *Baltimore Sun*, and the *Chicago Tribune*.

She serves as an entrepreneur in residence at the Polsky Center for Entrepreneurship and Innovation at the University of Chicago and on the governing board of the *Bulletin of the Atomic Scientists*.

She holds a bachelor's in journalism from Northwestern University, a master's in government from Johns Hopkins University, and an MBA from the University of Chicago's Booth School of Business.

Jenn Bane is a writer, producer, and the creative director of M. Harris & Co. She holds a bachelor's in journalism from Loyola University Chicago and was formerly employee No. 1 at Cards Against Humanity. Her former podcast *Friendshipping*, a feel-good advice show, was made into a book: *Friendshipping: The Art of Finding Friends, Making Friends, and Being Friends*. It is now available in bookstores and online.

Mark Jacob is the former associate managing editor for metro news for the *Chicago Tribune*. He was Mary Schmich's editor when she won the 2012 Pulitzer Prize for Commentary. Before joining the *Tribune*, he was Sunday editor at the *Chicago Sun-Times*. Illinois governor J.B. Pritzker appointed him to the state's Local Journalism Task Force, a legislatively mandated group studying financial support for the state's news outlets. A graduate of Hendrix College in Conway, Arkansas, Mark is the coauthor of nine books about history and photography.